ITALIAN HERITAGE DICTIONARY

ÉDITIONS RÉNYI INC.
355 Adelaide Street West, Suite 400, Toronto, Ontario Canada M5V 1S2

Italian Heritage Dictionary

Copyright © 1989 Éditions Rényi Inc.

Illustrated by Kathryn Adams, Pat Gangnon, Colin Gilles, David Shaw and Yvonne Zan

Designed by David Shaw and Associates

Cover illustration by Colin Gilles

Colour separations by New Concept Limited

Printed in Singapore

In this dictionary, as in reference work in general, no mention is made of patents, trademark rights, or other proprietary rights which may attach to certain words or entries. The absence of such mention, however, in no way implies that words or entries in question are exempt from such rights.

Typesetting by Osgoode Technical Translations, Ray's Typographics

English language editors: P. O'Brien-Hitching, R. LeBel, P. Renyi, K.C. Sheppard

Italian edition by A. Sarzotti, C. Pella

Italian Heritage Dictionary   ISBN 0-921606-24-9

INTRODUCTION

Some of Canada's best illustrators have contributed to this dictionary, which has been carefully designed to appeal to children, so that learning new words can be a pleasure.

Its unusually large number of terms – 3336 – makes the dictionary a flexible teaching tool. Because the vocabulary it encompasses is so broad, this dictionary can also be used to teach English as a Second Language to older children and adults, as well as helping young children acquire language skills.

NOTE TO TEACHERS AND PARENTS

In a children's dictionary, the most difficult decision is usually which words to include and which ones to leave out. Here, word selection has been based partly on word frequency analysis of English usage (in order to include the most commonly used terms), and partly on thematic clustering (in order to cover major fields of activity or interest).

This process was further complicated by the decision to systematically illustrate the meanings. Although the degree of abstraction has been kept reasonably low, it was deemed necessary to include terms such as "to expect" and "to forgive", which are virtually impossible to illustrate, given the space and other constraints. Instead of dropping these words, we decided to provide explanatory sentences that create a context.

Where variations occur between British and North-American English, both terms are given with an asterisk marking the British version (favor/favour*, gas/petrol*). Both variants are listed alphabetically in the index.

The alphabetical index at the end of the book lists every term in the dictionary with the number of its corresponding illustration. Teachers could use this feature to expand children's numeracy skills, by asking the child to match an index number with the actual illustration, as well as using it to train students in dictionary skills.

Great care has been taken to ensure that any contextual statements made are factual, have some educational value and are compatible with statements made elsewhere in the book. Lastly, from a strictly psychological viewpoint, the little girl featured in the book has not been made into a paragon of virtue; children will readily identify with her imperfections.

A te e a tutti i miei amici

Forse questo è il tuo primo dizionario italiano. . . Sono sicura che lo troverai divertente.

Io mi chiamo Sabrina. Vado a scuola volentieri e ho tanti amici. Al giovedì prendo lezioni di nuoto. Sono molto ghiotta. Ho un fratellino e ho le mie idee su tante cose. Se vuoi incontrare mio papà, che è un ammiraglio, guarda al fondo della pagina, verso destra. Mamma è alla pagina seguente, in alto. Se vuoi fare la mia conoscenza, devi cercare nel dizionario la parola "calm".

Vieni con me e scoprirai tante parole nuove e interessanti. Ti farai anche delle belle risate.

Le illustrazioni sono state disegnate da cinque persone adulte, che si sono divertite un mondo. Io le ho aiutate, disegnando una figura (quella della zebra). Ho anche scelto io l'ultima parola del dizionario: indovina quale è!

Questo dizionario è stato composto apposta per te, per i tuoi amici e le tue amichette. Spero che ti piacerà proprio tanto.

Sabrina

A

l'abbaco, il pallottoliere

1   abacus

di, circa, attorno

Parlami **di** tua madre.
Ci vuole **circa** un'ora.
Mario si guarda **attorno**.

Tell me about your mother.
It takes about an hour.
Mario looks about him.

2   about

La mela è **sopra** la sua testa.

3   above

Paolo è **assente** oggi.

4   absent

Questo è il pedale dell'**acceleratore**.

5   accelerator

un accento

John parla con **un accento** inglese.
Città ha l'**accento** sull'ultima vocale.

John speaks with a British accent.
Città has an accent on the last vowel.

6   accent

un incidente

7   accident

la fisarmonica

8   accordion

Tutti **accusano** Mirella.

9   to accuse

un asso di picche

10   ace

Mi **duole** la testa.

11   My head **aches.**

Un acido può bruciare la pelle.

12   acid

La ghianda è prodotta dalla quercia.

13   acorn

un'acrobata

14   acrobat

dirimpetto, attraverso

Paolo abita **dirimpetto** a me.
Francesca corre **attraverso** i campi.

Paolo lives across the street.
Francesca runs across the fields.

15   across

addizionare, fare l'addizione

16   to add

Questo è l'**indirizzo** di Sabrina.

17   address

Il papà di Sabrina è **un ammiraglio**.

18   admiral

Ernesto **adora** Sonia.

19   to adore

Gli adulti sono bambini cresciuti.

20   adult

Avanza il re!

21   to advance

Essere alti talvolta è **un vantaggio**.

22   advantage

La mamma di Sabrina ama **l'avventura**.

23   adventure

Filippo è **impaurito**.

24   He is afraid.

L'Africa è un continente.

25   Africa

dopo, dietro

Puoi giocare **dopo** cena.
Sta correndo **dietro** alla palla.

You can play after dinner.
He is running after the ball.

26   after

Il pomeriggio comincia a mezzogiorno.

27   afternoon

di nuovo, nuovamente

L'hai fatto **di nuovo**!
E' **nuovamente** il tuo turno!

You did it again!
It is your turn again.

28   again

Micio **si strofina** contro le gambe del signor Francesco.

29   to rub against

C'è una certa differenza d'**età**.

30   age

una persona **agile**

31   agile person

La caravella **si è arenata**.

32   aground

davanti, in anticipo

Elena è seduta **davanti** a Pierino.
Combina **in anticipo** per le tue vacanze!

Elena sits ahead of Pierino.
Plan ahead for your next holiday.

33   ahead

soccorrere, venire in aiuto

34   to provide aid

Cerca di **mirare** al bersaglio!

35   to aim

L'aquilone vola nell' **aria**.

36   air

Fido dorme sul **materassino pneumatico**.

37   air mattress

L'insetto è sotto una cupola **ermetica**.

38   airtight

Questo **aeroplano** sembra in difficoltà.

39   airplane/aeroplane*

Gli aerei atterrano all'**aeroporto**.

40   airport

Il passaggio separa le file di poltrone.

41   aisle

la sveglia

42   alarm clock

un albo fotografico

43   album

La casa è **in fiamme**.

44   alight

Certamente, uno dei pesci è **vivo**.

45   alive

Voglio **tutti** i dolci!

46   I want them **all**.

Un gatto in **un vicolo** cieco.

47   alley

un alligatore

48   alligator

la mandorla

49   almond

Baffo arriva **quasi** ad addentare l'osso.

50   almost

Perché è tutto **solo**?

51   alone

Camminano **lungo** il fiume.

52   along

forte, ad alta voce

53   aloud

l'alfabeto

*a b c d e f g h i l m n o
p q r s t u v z*

54   alphabet

Devo **già** andare via?

55   Do I have to go **already**?

Sto bene, non ho niente.

56   I am **alright**.

Anch' io ne voglio.

57   I **also** want some.

la scala **d'alluminio**

58   aluminum/aluminium* ladder

Cado **sempre**.

59   I **always** fall down.

un'ambulanza	un lupo **tra** gli agnelli	**un'ancora**	un monumento **antico**
60 ambulance	61 wolf **among** sheep	62 anchor	63 ancient
un angolo retto	Tito è **adirato.**	**gli animali**	**la caviglia**
64 angle	65 He is **angry.**	66 animals	67 ankle
annunciare	un **altro** panino	**La risposta** giusta è…	**la formica**
68 to **announce**	69 **another** sandwich	70 The **answer** is…	71 ant
l'Antartico	**un'antilope**	**le corna**	Non ho denaro.
72 Antarctic	73 antelope	74 antlers	75 I do not have **any** money.
Mangia **qualunque cosa**.	Tito non può andare **in nessun posto.**	Un acino è **separato** dal grappolo.	**la scimmia**
76 It eats **anything.**	77 He cannot go **anywhere.**	78 apart	79 ape

un alveare
80   apiary

chiedere scusa, scusarsi

Chiedere scusa significa dire: mi dispiace!
Scusate il mio ritardo!

To apologize is to say you are sorry.
I apologize for being late!

81   to apologize/apologise*

comparire, apparire

Il prestigiatore ha fatto **comparire** un coniglietto.
La regina è **apparsa** in televisione.

The magician made a rabbit appear.
The Queen appeared on television.

82   to appear

applaudire
83   to applaud

la mela
84   apple

il torsolo della mela
85   apple core

avvicinarsi
86   to approach

un'albicocca
87   apricot

In **aprile**, ogni goccia un barile!

88   April

il grembiule
89   apron

un acquario
90   aquarium

un arco
91   arch

un architetto
92   architect

Nell'**Artico** fa molto freddo.

93   Arctic

discutere
94   to argue

il braccio
95   arm

la poltrona
96   armchair

Lancillotto porta **l'armatura.**

97   armor/armour*

un'ascella
98   armpit

attorno, circa, verso

Attorno al mondo in ottanta giorni.
Un autocarro pesa **circa** 6 tonnellate.
Arriveremo **verso** mezzogiorno.

Around the world in eighty days
A truck weighs around 6 tons.
We will be there around noon.

99   around

disporre i fiori

100　　to **arrange** flowers

Il poliziotto **arresta** Tito.

101　　to **arrest**

arrivare

102　　to **arrive**

la **freccia**

103　　arrow

il **carciofo**

104　　artichoke

un **artista**

105　　artist

Come puoi vedere, Sabrina è
cresciuta.
Fa' **come** ti dico!
Ho **tanto** denaro **quanto** ne
ha lui.

As you can see
Do as I tell you!
I have as much money as he.

106　　as

la **cenere**

107　　ash

il **portacenere**

108　　ashtray

L'Asia è un continente.

109　　Asia

chiedere informazioni
sulla strada da prendere

110　　to **ask** for directions

Gloria e Puffina sono
addormentate.

111　　asleep

gli **asparagi**

112　　asparagus

Prendi due **aspirine**!

113　　aspirin

Nico **ha stupito** Luisa.

114　　to **astonish**

un **astronauta**

115　　astronaut

l'**astronomo**

116　　astronomer

a

Elena è **a** casa con suo papà.
Guardano il quadro.
Li vedrò **a** Pasqua.

Elena is at home with her dad.
They are looking at the picture.
I will see them at Easter.

117　　at

un'**atleta**

118　　athlete

un **atlante**

119　　atlas

l'atmosfera della terra	**un atomo**	**attaccare**	Fa' **attenzione!**
120 atmosphere	121 atom	122 to attach	123 Pay attention!
Cosa tieni in **soffitta?**	Il giocoliere diverte **il pubblico**.	**Agosto** è il mese delle ferie.	**La zia** è sorella di mia mamma.
124 attic	125 audience	126 August	127 My **aunt** is my mother's sister.
L'Australia è un continente.	**un autore**	una sveglia **automatica**	In **autunno** cadono le foglie.
128 Australia	129 author	130 automatic	131 autumn
la valanga	**un avocado**	Indovina perché Tito è **sveglio!!!**	Lei è andata **via**.
132 avalanche	133 avocado	134 awake	135 She is **away**.
un odore **terribile**	una persona **sgraziata**	**un'ascia**	**L'asse** collega le due ruote.
136 an **awful** smell	137 an **awkward** person	138 axe	139 axle

Che carino questo **bambino**!

la carrozzina

Grattami **la schiena**!

140　　　baby

141　baby carriage/pram*

142　　　back

uova e **pancetta**

Questa mela è **bacata**.

il distintivo

**indietreggiare,
fare marcia indietro**

144　bacon and eggs

145　　bad apple

146　　　badge

143　　to back up

Che cosa c'è nella **borsa**?

L'esca attira il topo.

cuocere, cuocere al forno

Il fornaio fa il pane.

147　　　bag

148　　　bait

149　　to bake

150　　　baker

la panetteria

L'acrobata si tiene in
equilibrio sulla corda.

il balcone

Battista è **calvo**.

151　　bakery

152　good balance

153　　balcony

154　　　bald

la palla

la ballerina

il balletto

il palloncino

155　　　ball

156　　ballerina

157　　ballet

158　　balloon

un pallone aerostatico, una mongolfiera

159   hot air **balloon**

la banana

160   banana

il nastro

161   band

un'orchestra

162   musical **band**

La benda ha fatto passare il male.

163   bandage

battere

164   to **bang**

Rino scende scivolando sul **corrimano**.

165   banister

Rosvaldo porta i suoi soldi in **banca**.

166   bank

una sbarra di ferro

167   bar

I bar sono riservati agli adulti.

168   bar/pub*

il filo spinato

169   barbed wire

Il barbiere taglia i capelli a Michele.

170   barber

un piede **nudo**

171   one **bare** foot

il fienile, la stalla

172   bargain

la chiatta

173   barge

abbaiare

174   to **bark**

L'orzo cresce nei campi.

176   barley

il capannone agricolo, il fienile

177   barn

I soldati abitano in **una caserma**.

178   barracks

la corteccia di un albero

175   bark

un barile d'olio d'oliva
179   barrel

la canna della pistola
180   barrel

la molletta
181   barrette/hair slide*

la sbarra di un passaggio a livello
182   barrier

la base della colonna
183   base

una base del gioco del baseball
184   base

il baseball
185   baseball

il seminterrato
186   basement/cellar*

il basilico
187   basil

il canestro
188   basket

la pallacanestro
189   basketball

due **mazze** da gioco
190   bats

Sto facendo **il bagno**.
192   I am having a **bath**.

il bagno
193   bathroom

la vasca da bagno
194   bathtub

Il pipistrello vola di notte.
191   bat

una pila per la tua radiolina
195   battery

La barca veleggia nella **baia**.
196   bay

La mamma usa **le foglie d'alloro** per l'arrosto.
197   bay leaves

il bazar
198   bazaar

essere

Prometti di **essere** buona?
Sono buona!
Pierino e Luca **sono** bravi,
ma Sabrina **è** brava?

Do you promise to be good?
I am good.
Pierino and Luca are good,
but is Sabrina good?

199   to **be**

---

la spiaggia

200   beach

---

una perla della collana

201   bead

---

il becco

202   beak

---

un raggio di luce

203   **beam** of light

---

i fagioli

204   beans

Quest'**orso** sa andare in bicicletta.

205   bear

---

una barba molto lunga

206   beard

---

una bestia orribile,
una bestiaccia

207   beast

Marina **batte** il tamburo.

208   to **beat**

Fufi è **bella**!

209   beautiful

---

il castoro

210   beaver

Piango **perché**...

211   I am crying **because**...

---

diventare

Il bruco

diventa

una farfalla

212   to **become**

---

il letto

213   bed

---

la lampada da notte

214 bed lamp/reading light*

---

la camera da letto

215   bedroom

Le api vivono in **un alveare**.

216   bee

---

il faggio

217   beech

L'ape è un insetto molto utile.

218   beehive

un boccale di **birra**

219   beer

Le barbabietole crescono sotto terra.

220   beet/beetroot*

lo scarafaggio

221   beetle

Lavati le mani **prima** di cena.

222   Wash your hands **before** dinner.

mendicare

223   to **beg**

cominciare

Tanto per **cominciare**, facciamo colazione!
La lezione di piano di Sabrina **comincia** alle nove.

To begin with, let's have breakfast!
Sabrina's piano lesson begins at nine.

224   to **begin**

Chiara **si comporta** bene.

225   to **behave**

Giulia si nasconde **dietro** l'albero.

226   behind

beige

227   beige

Io credo ai dragoni.

228   I **believe** in dragons.

la campana

229   bell

l'ombelico

230   belly button

Questo cane mi **appartiene**.

231   He **belongs** to me.

Il gatto è **sotto** la tavola.

232   below

la cintura

233   belt

la panchina

234   bench

una **curva** della strada

235   bend

piegare

236   to **bend**

il berretto

237   beret

Patrizia è **accanto** all'albero.

238   beside

inoltre, oltre a

Inoltre, non dovresti mangiare tanto zucchero!
C'erano molti altri studenti, **oltre a** lui.

Besides, you should not eat so much sugar!
There were many other pupils besides him.

239   besides

la migliore

240   best

meglio, migliore

Giulia scrive **meglio** di Davide.
Questo libro è **migliore** del primo.

Giulia writes better than Davide.
This book is better than the first one.

241   better

Filippo cammina **tra** due massi.

242   between

il bavaglino

243   bib

la bicicletta

244   bicycle

grande

245   big

La bici è una bicicletta.

246   bike

il **biglietto** di banca

247   bill/banknote*

il cartellone pubblicitario

248   billboard/hoarding*

il gioco del **biliardo**

249   billiards/snooker*

legare

250   to bind/tie up*

il binocolo

251   binoculars

un uccello

252   bird

la nascita

Sabrina pesava tre chilogrammi alla **nascita**.
Debora è italiana di **nascita**.

Sabrina weighed three kilograms at birth.
Debra is Italian by birth.

253   birth

Buon **compleanno**!

254   birthday

il biscotto

255   biscuit

Franco **addenta** il panino.

256   to bite

Ha preso un grosso **boccone**.

257   bite

amaro

La birra ha un gusto **amaro**.
Sabrina versò **amare** lacrime quando perse la sua bambola preferita.

Beer has a bitter taste.
Sabrina wept bitter tears when she lost her favorite doll.

258   bitter

nero	la mora	il merlo	Anna ha fatto un disegno sulla **lavagna**.
259 black	260 blackberry	261 blackbird	262 blackboard

il ribes	il fabbro	La lama è tagliente!	incolpare, biasimare
263 blackcurrant	264 blacksmith	265 blade	Papà ha **incolpato** Sabrina d'aver rotto il vaso, ma lei non lo aveva fatto. Papà dovrebbe **biasimare** Davide. *Dad blamed Sabrina for breaking the vase, but she did not do it. Dad should blame Davide.* 266 to blame

una pagina **bianca**	la coperta	Uno scoppio è un'esplosione.	far saltare
267 **blank** page	268 blanket	269 blast	270 to blast

L'incendio sta divampando.	la giacca sportiva, il blazer	La candeggina serve a sbiancare i panni.	Le sanguina il naso.
271 blaze	272 blazer	273 bleach	274 to bleed

un'omogeneizzatore	Un cieco non può vedere.	Franca sbatte le palpebre.	Le vesciche sono dolorose.
275 blender	276 blind	277 to blink	278 blister

una bufera di neve	**il cubo**	**un isolato**	Il poliziotto lo **ha bloccato**.
279 blizzard	280 block	281 block	282 to block
i capelli **biondi**	una trasfusione di **sangue**	Questa pianta è in piena **fioritura.**	In primavera gli alberi **fioriscono.**
283 blond/blonde*	284 blood	285 bloom	286 to blossom
una macchia d'inchiostro	**la camicetta**	**una botta** in testa	**soffiare**
287 blot	288 blouse	289 a **blow** to the head	290 to blow
azzurro	**i mirtilli**	**smussato, brusco**	Stefania **arrossisce** facilmente.
291 blue	292 blueberries	Questo coltello è troppo **smussato** per tagliare i pomodori. Chiara fu molto **brusca** con lui. *This knife is too blunt to cut the tomatoes. Chiara was very blunt with him.* 293 blunt	294 to blush
il cinghiale	**una tavola** di legno	**vantarsi**	**la barca** a remi
295 boar	296 board	Fabio **si vanta** sempre. Non puo **vantarsi** di essere modesto. *Fabio is always boasting. His modesty is nothing to boast about.* 297 to boast	298 boat

una forcina da capelli _299_ bobby pin/hairgrip*	**il corpo** umano _300_ body	**bollire** _301_ to boil	**il bullone** _302_ bolt
un osso per il cane _303_ bone	**il falò** _304_ bonfire	**il libro** _305_ book	**uno scaffale** per i libri _306_ bookshelf
il boomerang _307_ boomerang	**lo stivale** _308_ boot	**il confine, la frontiera** _309_ border	Il cemento è difficile da **perforare**. _310_ to bore

nato

In che anno sei **nata**?
E' un poeta **nato**.

What year were you born?
He is a born poet.

_312_   born

prendere in prestito

Sabrina sovente **prende in prestito** la bicicletta di suo fratello.
Posso **prendere in prestito** il tuo libro?

Sabrina often borrows her brother's bike.
Can I borrow your book?

_313_   to borrow

il padrone

_314_   boss

annoiare

Sabrina qualche volta **annoia** da morire.
Luca mi **annoia**, perché parla troppo.

Sabrina can bore people to death.
Luca bores me because he talks too much.

_311_   to bore

ambedue, sia...che

Enzo e Renato sono **ambedue** graziosi.
Sia l'uno **che** l'altro hanno un bel sorriso.

Enzo and Renato are both cute.
Both have a nice smile.

_315_   both

la bottiglietta

_316_   bottle

un apribottiglie

_317_   bottle opener

il fondo dell'acquario

_318_   bottom

il masso

319   boulder

la palla **rimbalza**

320   to **bounce**

il mazzo di fiori

321   bouquet

l'arco e le frecce

322   bow

la scodella, la ciotola

324   bowl

C'è qualcosa nella **scatola.**

325   box

il pugile

326   boxer

la cravatta a farfalla, il papillon

323   bow tie

il ragazzo

327   boy

il reggipetto

328   bra

il braccialetto

329   bracelet

vantarsi

Noemi **si vanta** dei suoi nuovi giocattoli.
Suo papà le dice di non **vantarsi.**

Noemi brags about her new toys.
Her dad tells her not to brag.

330   to **brag**

il cervello

331   brain

Per fermare la macchina si usa il pedale del **freno.**

332   brake

frenare

333   to brake

il ramo dell'albero

334   branch

coraggioso

Il dentista dice che sei stata molto **coraggiosa,** Sabrina.

The dentist says you were very brave, Sabrina.

335   brave

il pane

336   bread

La palla **ha rotto** la lampada.

337   to **break**

La macchina **si è rotta.**

338   to **break down**

Il ladro **ha scassinato** la gioielleria.	la **colazione**
339 to **break** in	340 breakfast
Che **alito** cattivo!	**respirare**
341 breath	342 to breathe

La tua casa è fatta di **mattoni**?	Questo **muratore** si chiama Pamela.
343 brick	344 bricklayer
La sposa è un po' timida.	Anche **lo sposo** è timido.
345 bride	346 bridegroom

il **ponte**	la **briglia** del cavallo
347 bridge	348 bridle
la **borsa** di cuoio	Il sole è **splendente**.
349 briefcase	350 **bright** sun

Baffo mi **porta** le ciabatte.	Sabrina **riporta** i libri alla biblioteca.
351 to bring	352 to bring back
un vetro **fragile**	i **broccoli**
353 brittle glass	354 broccoli

la **spilla**	**Un ruscello** è un fiume piccolino.
355 brooch	356 brook
la **scopa**	Voglio bene a mio **fratello**.
357 broom	358 I love my **brother**.

il sopracciglio

359   brow

marrone

360   brown

Angelo ha bisogno di
spazzolarsi i capelli.

362   to brush

la spazzola

363   brush

Che brutto **livido**!

361   bruise

i cavolini di Bruxelles

366   brussels sprouts

il pennello

364   paintbrush

lo spazzolino da denti

365   toothbrush

A Susanna il bagno piace
con tante **bolle** di sapone.

367   bubble

il secchio

368   bucket

la fibbia della cintura

369   belt buckle

il bocciolo

370   bud

il bisonte

371   buffalo

un insetto

372   bug

la tromba dei soldati

373   bugle

costruire

374   to build

il toro

375   bull

il bulldozer

376   bulldozer

Le pallottole sono molto
pericolose.

377   bullet

il megafono

378 bullhorn/megaphone*

Leone è un **attaccabrighe**.

379   bully

Osvaldo ha **un bernoccolo** sulla testa.

380   bump

i paraurti

381   bumpers

un mazzo di asparagi

382   bunch

una fascina di legna da ardere

383   bundle

la boa

384   buoy

lo scassinatore

385   burglar

bruciare, ardere

386   to burn

Il palloncino è **scoppiato**.

387   to burst

sotterrare

388   to bury

un autobus

389   bus

la fermata dell'autobus

390   bus stop

Un cespuglio è più piccolo di un albero.

391   bush

In questo momento sono **occupato**.

392   I am busy now.

ma

Vorrei andare, **ma** sono impegnato.
Paolo è alto, **ma** sua sorella è più alta di lui.

I would like to go, but I am busy.
Paolo is tall, but his sister is taller.

393   but

il macellaio

394   butcher

Spalmo **il burro** sul pane.

395   butter

la farfalla

396   butterfly

i bottoni

397   buttons

Filippo si **compra** un gelato.

398   to buy

C

il cavolo

399   cabbage

una piccola, dolce **capanna**

400   cabin

un armadietto

401   cabinet

il cavo

402   cable/lead*

il cactus

403   cactus

la gabbia per gli uccelli

404   cage

la torta

405   cake

la calcolatrice

406   calculator

il calendario

407   calendar

Il vitello è il piccolo della mucca.

408   calf

chiamare

409   to **call**

Sabrina è sempre **calma**.

412   She is **calm**.

il cammello

413   camel

la macchina fotografica

414   camera

cancellare

Cancelleremo il picnic se pioverà.
Sabrina **ha cancellato** la nostra gita allo zoo.

*We will call off the picnic if it rains.
Sabrina has called off our trip to the zoo.*

410   to **call off**

Luca ed Enrico **campeggiano** da soli.

415   to **camp**

il campeggio

416   campsite

la lattina

417   can

chiamare al telefono

411   to **call up**/to **phone***

un apriscatole
418 can opener/tin* opener

La chiatta passa attraverso **un canale.**
419 canal

il canarino
420 canary

la candela
421 candle

il candelabro
422 candlestick

i dolciumi, le caramelle
423 candy/sweets*

Cammina con **la canna.**
424 cane/walking stick*

il cannone
425 cannon

Non riesco a vedere.
426 I cannot see.

la canoa
427 canoe

il melone
428 cantaloupe

Il fiume scorre al fondo di **un canyon.**
429 canyon

il berretto
430 cap

La nave sta aggirando **il capo.**
431 cape

la cappa del moschettiere
432 cape

una lettera **maiuscola**

A

433 capital

il capitano della nave
434 captain

catturare una farfalla
435 to capture

l'automobile, la macchina
436 car

La carovana attraversa il deserto.
437 caravan

le carte

438   cards

la scatola di **cartone**

439   cardboard

L'infermiera si **prende cura** dei malati.

440   to **care**

Sebastiano è **sconsiderato**

441   He is **careless.**

il **carico** dell'aereo

442   cargo

i garofani

443   carnation

Carnevale, che allegria!

444   carnival

il falegname

445   carpenter

il tappeto

446   carpet

la carrozzina

447   carriage/pram*

la carota

448   carrot

Il Signor Fortini **porta** una grossa cassa.

449   to **carry**

il carretto

450   cart

Le viti sono confezionate in **scatole** da 100.

451   carton

trinciare un pollo

452   to **carve**

il baule

453   case

denaro contante

454   cash

noci di acagiù

455   cashew nuts

il castello

456   castle

il gatto

457   cat

il catalogo

458   catalog/catalogue*

afferrare

459   to catch

Guglielmo **ha raggiunto** Olga.

460   to catch up with

il bruco

461   caterpillar

una mandra di **bovini**

462   cattle

la caldaia

463   cauldron

il cavolfiore

464   cauliflower

la cavalleria

465   cavalry

Pensi che ci sia un orso nella **caverna**?

466   cave

il soffitto

467   ceiling

festeggiare

468   to celebrate

il sedano

469   celery

Il tuo corpo è fatto di **cellule** come questa.

470   cell

il seminterrato

471   cellar

il cemento

472   cement

il centro del cerchio

473   center/centre*

Ci sono 100 **centimetri** in un metro.

474   centimeter/centimetre*

il millepiedi

475   centipede

il secolo

Ci sono 100 anni in **un secolo**.

There are one hundred years in a century.

476   century

i fiocchi d'avena, di frumento.

477   cereal

certo

Sabrina è **certa** d'aver ragione.
Sabrina prova un **certo** sentimento per Filippo.

Sabrina is certain that she is right.
Sabrina has a certain feeling for Filippo.

478   certain

il certificato

479   certificate

la catena

480   chain

la sega a motore

481   chainsaw

la sedia

482   chair

Il **gesso** serve a scrivere sulla lavagna.

483   chalk

la campionessa

484   champion

gli spiccioli

485   change

un **canale** navigabile

487   channel

Questo è **il** dodicesimo **capitolo** del libro.

488   chapter

il carattere

Sabrina ha un **caratterino**.
Che cosa significa questo **carattere** cinese?

Sabrina has a strong character.
What does this Chinese character mean?

489   character

Carlo **si è cambiato** i vestiti.

486   to change

il carbone di legna

490   charcoal

il cardo

491   chard

accusare, ricaricare

La polizia **ha accusato** Tito di furto.
Il tuo giocattolo si è fermato perchè mi sono scordato di **ricaricare** la batteria.

The police charged Tito with robbery.
Your toy has stopped because I forgot to charge the battery.

492   to charge

il cocchio

493   chariot

il grafico

494   chart

rincorrere

495   to chase

chiacchierare

496   to chat

una matita **a buon mercato**, una corona molto cara

497   **cheap** pencil, expensive crown

Nico **imbroglia**, perché sta copiando.

498   to cheat

controllare, depositare

Hai controllato le tue addizioni?
Favorite **depositare** il cappotto all'entrata.

*Did you check your addition?
Check your coat at the entrance, please.*

499   to check

la guancia

500   cheek

Il formaggio si ricava dal latte.

501   cheese

un assegno

502   cheque*/check

le ciliegie

503   cherries

a **petto** nudo

504   chest

una castagna

505   chestnut

Mastica bene prima di inghiottire.

506   to chew

i ceci

507   chick peas

il pollo

508   chicken

la varicella

509   chicken-pox

Il capo saluta i suoi soldati.

510   chief

la bambina

511   child

una giornata **rigida**

512   a chilly day

il camino

513   chimney

lo scimpanzè

514   chimpanzee

il mento

515   chin

tazze e piattini di **porcellana**

516   china/crockery*

una scheggia di legno

517   chip

Lo scultore usa **uno scalpello**.

518   chisel

l'erba cipollina

519   chives

una tavoletta di **cioccolato**

520   chocolate

il coro

521   choir

Strangolare qualcuno non è uno scherzo.

522   to choke

Gianni **si sente soffocare**: ha inghiottito un osso.

523   to choke on

Quale dei due devo **scegliere**?

524   to choose

tritare

525   to chop

i bastoncini per mangiare

526   chopsticks

Il paraurti dell'auto è rivestito di **cromo.**

527   chrome

i crisantemi

528   chrysanthemum

un pezzo di carbone

529   a chunk/lump* of coal

Il fumo di quel **sigaro** puzza.

530   cigar

La sigaretta fa male alla salute.

531   cigarette

il circolo, il cerchio

532   circle

il circo

533   circus

Abiti in una grande **città**?

534   city

Il mollusco vive nella sua conchiglia.

535   clam

La morsa tiene i due pezzi insieme.

536   clamp

applaudire

537   to clap

l'aula scolastica

538   classroom

Il granchio ha chele molto robuste.

539   claw

---

l'argilla

L'argilla si usa per fare i mattoni.
Si possono anche fare vasi e piatti con **l'argilla**.

Clay is used to make bricks. You can also make pots and dishes out of clay.

540   clay

La bambina è **pulita**.

541   She is all **clean**.

Zia Anna **sparecchia** la tavola.

542   to clear

---

la rupe

543   cliff

---

arrampicarsi, scalare

544   to climb

---

la clinica

545   clinic

---

tagliare

546   to clip

---

un orologio da tavolo

547   clock

Nina **chiude** il libro.

548   to close

Il tuo **guardaroba** è in ordine?

549   closet/cupboard*

---

la stoffa, lo strofinaccio

I vestiti sono fatti di **stoffa**.
La mamma usa uno **strofinaccio** da cucina per lavare i piatti.

Clothes are made out of cloth. Mother uses a dishcloth to wipe the dishes.

550   cloth

---

i vestiti

551   clothes

---

il filo per stendere i panni

552   clothes line

---

la nuvola

553   cloud

Un trifoglio con quattro foglie porta fortuna.

554   clover

---

il pagliaccio

555   clown

Thal usa **la clava** per cacciare.

556   club

---

l'indizio, il suggerimento

La polizia ha trovato **un indizio** per il delitto.
Ti darò un **suggerimento**.

*The police found a clue to the crime.
I will give you a clue.*

557   clue

Per inserire la marcia, si schiaccia **la frizione.**

558   clutch

Afferra la corda!

559   to **clutch**

E' il nostro **allenatore.**

560   coach

Abbiamo viaggiato in **corriera.**

561   coach

Il **carbone** viene estratto nelle miniere.

563   coal

ruvido, grossolano

Questa stoffa è molto **ruvida.** Non usare parole **grossolane!**

This cloth is very coarse. *Do not use coarse language!*

564   coarse

la costa

565   coast

allenare

Teresa **allena** la squadra due volte alla settimana.

Teresa coaches the team twice a week.

562   to **coach**

D'inverno occorre **un cappotto** pesante.

566   coat

Il ragno tesse **la ragnatela.**

567   cobweb

una tazza di **cacao** caldo

568   cocoa

la noce di cocco

569   coconut

il merluzzo

570   cod

Con questi chicchi si fa del buon **caffè.**

571   coffee

la cassa da morto

572   coffin

la serpentina

573   coil

la moneta

574   coin

Ho **freddo.**

575   I am **cold.**

il colletto

576   collar

La sorella di Sabrina **colleziona** francobolli.

577   to **collect**

Il collegio è una scuola per studenti grandi.

578   college

Le automobili **si scontrano** se i guidatori s'addormentano.

579   to collide

uno scontro frontale

580   collision

Qual'è **il colore** che preferisci?

581   color/colours*

una cavalla col suo **puledro**

582   colt

due **colonne** di marmo

583   column

il pettine

584   comb

Sandra **si pettina** i capelli.

585   to comb

mescolare gli ingredienti

586   combine

venire

Sabrina **è venuta** alla festa in autobus.
Dile di **venire** a casa!

Sabrina came to the party by bus.
Tell her to come home.

587   to come

La maniglia **si è staccata.**

588   to come off

E' svenuto, ma **si sta riprendendo.**

589   to come to

comodo

590   comfortable

Una virgola in realtà non è cosi grossa.

591   comma

comandare, dare un comando

592   to command

la comunità

La scuola è stata costruita con l'impegno dell'intera **comunità.**

The school was built thanks to the effort of the entire community.

593   community

due **compagni** inseparabili

594   companion

Sono in buona **compagnia.**

595   I am in good **company.**

paragonare

596   to compare

La mia **bussola** indica il nord.

597   My **compass** points north.

Gian Giacomo **ha composto** un'opera.

598　to compose

il compositore

599　composer

una composizione per pianoforte

600　composition

un calcolatore elettronico

601　computer

Monica **si concentra** sul suo lavoro.

602　to concentrate

il concerto

603　concert

il cemento

604　concrete

il direttore d'orchestra

605　conductor

il cono

607　cone

il cono di gelato

608　ice cream **cone**

la pigna

609　pine **cone**

il controllore dei biglietti sul treno

606　conductor/guard*

L'acrobata è **sicuro di sè**.

610　confident

Sono un po' **confuso**.

611　I am confused.

congratularsi con il vincitore

612　to congratulate

connettere

613　to connect

la consonante

B, c, d, f, g, sono delle **consonanti**.

B, c, d, f, g are consonants.

614　consonant

Questa **donna poliziotto** ti può aiutare.

615　constable

Una costellazione comprende molte stelle.

616　constellation

I continenti sono sette.

617　continent

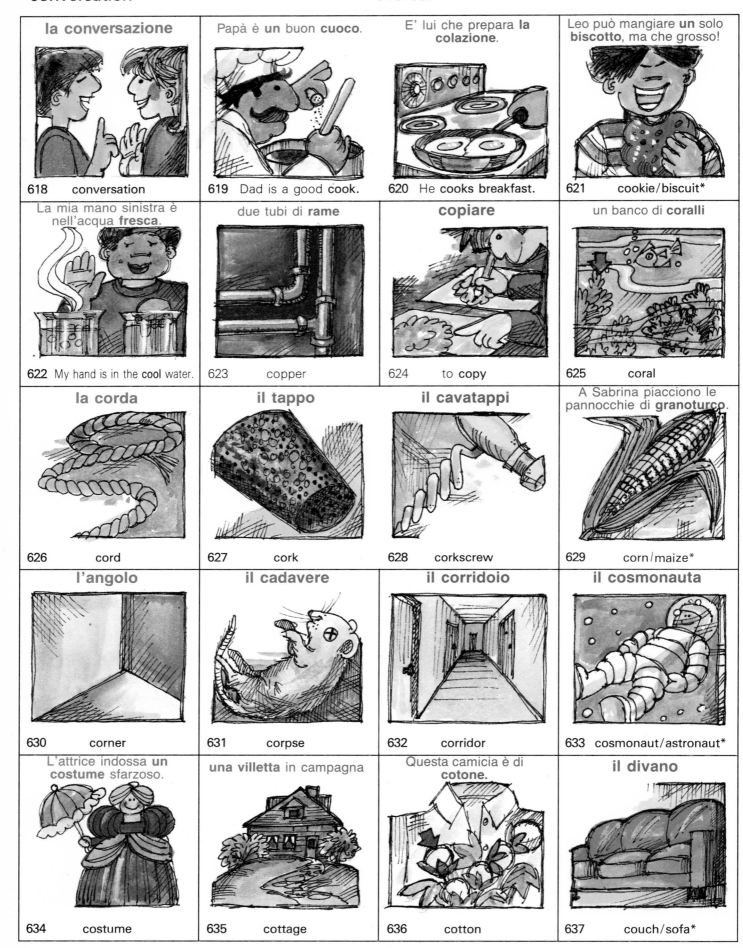

la conversazione	Papà è **un** buon **cuoco**.	E' lui che prepara **la colazione**.	Leo può mangiare **un** solo **biscotto**, ma che grosso!
618 conversation	619 Dad is a good **cook**.	620 He **cooks** breakfast.	621 cookie/biscuit*
La mia mano sinistra è nell'acqua **fresca**.	due tubi di **rame**	**copiare**	un banco di **coralli**
622 My hand is in the **cool** water.	623 copper	624 to **copy**	625 coral
la corda	**il tappo**	**il cavatappi**	A Sabrina piacciono le pannocchie di **granoturco**.
626 cord	627 cork	628 corkscrew	629 corn/maize*
l'angolo	**il cadavere**	**il corridoio**	**il cosmonauta**
630 corner	631 corpse	632 corridor	633 cosmonaut/astronaut*
L'attrice indossa **un costume** sfarzoso.	**una villetta** in campagna	Questa camicia è di **cotone**.	**il divano**
634 costume	635 cottage	636 cotton	637 couch/sofa*

638 Livia **tossisce** educatamente.
to cough

639 **contare**
to count

640 **il contatore**
counter

641 Mettilo sul **banco**!
counter

642 Vai spesso in **campagna**?
country

643 Questo **paese** è il Canada.
country

644 Mamma e papà fanno **una** bella **coppia.**
couple

645 Ci vuole **un bel coraggio** per combattere un drago.
courage

646 **il campo** da tennis
court

647 **La** mia **cugina** è figlia dello zio Carlo.
My cousin is my uncle's daughter.

648 **coprire**
to cover

649 **il coperchio**
cover

650 **la mucca, la vacca**
cow

651 Questo ragazzo è **un codardo.**
This boy is a **coward.**

652 **il cow-boy**
cowboy

653 **un** grosso **granchio**
crab

654 Il vaso ha **un'incrinatura.**
crack

655 **il cracker**
cracker

656 **la culla**
cradle

657 **La gru** è un uccello migratore.
crane

una gru in un cantiere edile

658   crane

schiantarsi, scontrarsi

659   to **crash**

Che cosa c'è nella **gabbia**?

660   crate

camminare carponi, strisciare

661   to **crawl**

il gambero

662   crayfish

i pastelli, le matite colorate

663   crayons

la panna, la crema

A papà piacè **la panna** nel caffè.
La **crema** solare previene le scottature.

Dad likes cream in his coffee.
Sun cream prevents sunburn.

664   cream

la piega

665   crease

Che strana **creatura**!

666   creature

Un torrente è un piccolo fiume.

667   creek

l'equipaggio della nave

668   the **crew**

un lettino per bimbi

669   crib/cot*

il grillo

670   cricket

un criminale dietro le sbarre

671   criminal

il coccodrillo

672   crocodile

Quando spunta **il croco**, la primavera è alle porte.

673   crocus

Quell'imbrogliona ha rubato una mela.

674   crook

un palo **storto**

675   **crooked** post

La torre è diritta, ma il quadro è **inclinato**.

676 **crooked** painting, upright tower

un buon **raccolto**

677   crop

la croce

678   cross

Guarda prima di **attraversare**.

679   to cross

Il 6 è **cancellato**.

680   to cross out

il corvo

681   crow

Che **folla** in così poco spazio!

682   A big **crowd** in a small space.

la corona

683   crown

Messer Baldo **incorona** la nuova regina.

684   to crown

le briciole

685   crumb

Per fare il vino, Ermenegildo **pigia** l'uva.

686   to crush

Sabrina preferisce **la crosta**.

687   crust

la gruccia

688   crutch

piangere

689   to cry

una sfera di **cristallo**

690   crystal

il cucciolo di un'orsa

691   cub

il cubo

692   cube

il cuculo

693   cuckoo

il cetriolo

694   cucumber

il polsino della camicia

695   cuff

una tazza di tè

696   cup

La brocca è sulla **credenza**.

697   cupboard

il cordone del marciapiede

698   curb/kerb*

Sono **guarito**!

699   I am **cured**.

Samanta **si arriccia** i capelli.

700   to **curl**

Ora i suoi capelli sono **ricci**.

701   curly

Elena è **curiosa**.

702   curious

il ribes

703   currant

La corrente è molto forte.

704   current

le tende

705   curtains

la curva

706   curve

il cuscino

707   cushion

il cliente

708   customer

tagliare, affettare

709   to **cut**

Sandra è **carina**.

712   cute/sweet*

le posate

713   cutlery

la bicicletta

714   cycle

tagliare la strada

710   to **cut in**

il cilindro

715   cylinder

i cimbali

716   cymbals

Il cipresso è una pianta alta e sottile.

717   cypress

Ritagliare una bambola di carta.

711   to **cut out**

La giunchiglia fiorisce in primavera.

718   daffodil

il pugnale

719   dagger

un giornale **quotidiano**

720   daily

un'azienda che produce latte

721   dairy

Sfogliamo insieme **una margherita**.

722   daisy

Una diga sbarra il fiume.

723   dam

un pacco **danneggiato**

724   damaged

umido

725   damp

danzare, **ballare**

726   to **dance**

la ballerina

727   dancer

Il dente di leone è un'erbaccia dannosa.

728   dandelion

Attenzione, **pericolo**!

729   danger

Leone non ha paura del **buio**.

730   dark

il gioco dei **dardi**

731   dart

il cruscotto

732   dashboard

Qual'è **la data** di oggi?

733   date

E' mia **figlia** Grazia.

734   daughter

l'inizio di **una** bella **giornata**

735   the start of a nice **day**

un topo **morto**

736   **dead** mouse

I sordi non ci sentono.

737   deaf

---

caro

Carlo è un **caro** amico.
Cara mamma, al campeggio
mi diverto tanto.

Carlo is a dear friend.
Dear Mom, camp is fun!

738   dear

Dicembre è l'ultimo mese
dell'anno.

739   December

---

decidere

Sabrina non riesce a
decidere che cosa indossare.
Forse la mamma dovrà
decidere per lei.

Sabrina cannot decide what to wear.
Mom may have to decide for her.

740   to decide

---

il ponte della nave

741   deck

Il pirata **decora** l'albero di Natale.

742   to decorate

---

la decorazione

743   decoration

Alberto evita il lato
profondo della piscina.

744   deep end

C'è **un cervo** nella foresta!

745   deer

---

consegnare

746   to deliver

Battista mi **ha ammaccato**
la macchina.

747   to dent

---

la dentista

748   dentist

---

un grande magazzino

749   department store

---

il deserto

750   desert

Chi mi ha messo **la
scrivania** nel deserto?

751   desk

---

il dessert

752   dessert

Godzilla **distrugge** la città.

753   to destroy

Il cacciatorpediniere è una
nave militare.

754   destroyer

---

l'investigatore

755   detective

Al mattino le foglie sono
coperte di **rugiada**.

756   dew

la diagonale
757   diagonal

il diagramma
758   diagram

il diamante
759   diamond

I bebè hanno bisogno di **pannolini.**
760   diaper/nappy*

Tieni **un diario**?
761   diary

Sta cercando una parola nel **dizionario**.
762   dictionary

morire
763   to die

differenza

Tutti nascono uguali, non c'è nessuna **differenza.**
C'è molta **differenza** tra la notte e il giorno.

All people are born equal, there is no difference.
There is quite a difference between night and day.

764   difference

gente **diversa**
765   different people

vangare
766   to dig

Il serpente **digerisce** un elefante.
767   The snake **digests** an elephant.

La luce nella stanza è **fioca**.
768   dim

Sabrina ha due **fossette** nelle guance.
769   dimple

il canotto
770   dinghy

la sala da pranzo
771   dining room

una cena a luce di candela
772   dinner

il dinosauro
773   dinosaur

La direzione è questa!
774   direction

Papà ha camminato tra **l'immondizia.**
775   dirt

I suoi pantaloni sono **sporchi.**
776   dirty

Non sono d'accordo con te.	La mela è **sparita**.	L'incendio è stato **un** vero **disastro**.	**scoprire**
777 to **disagree**	778 to **disappear**	779 **disaster**	780 to **discover**
discutere	**la malattia**	Sabrina indossa **un travestimento**.	Sabrina… ci sono **i piatti** da lavare!
781 to **discuss**	782 **disease**	783 **disguise**	784 **dishes**
una persona **disonesta**	**la risciacquatura** dei piatti	A Marina piace la verdura, ma **detesta** i broccoli.	La pastiglia **si scioglie** nell'acqua.
785 a **dishonest** person	786 **dishwater**	787 to **dislike**	788 to **dissolve**
la distanza tra i due alberi	Quell'albero è molto **distante**.	**il quartiere** in cui abito	scavare **un fossato**
789 **distance** between two trees	790 a **distant** tree	791 **district**	792 **ditch**
tuffarsi	**dividere** una mela in due	**Ho il capogiro.**	Devo **fare** qualcosa per aggiustare lo sgabello.
793 to **dive**	794 to **divide**	795 I feel **dizzy**.	796 What shall I **do**?

il pontile	**il dottore**	**il cane**	**la bambola**
797 dock	798 doctor	799 dog	800 doll
il delfino	**la cupola**	Farfarello è **un asino** fortissimo.	**la porta**
801 dolphin	802 dome	803 donkey	804 door
la maniglia	**doppio**	**la pasta**	**La colomba** è il simbolo della pace.
805 doorknob	806 double	807 dough	808 dove
Sabrina ha un cuscino di **piume.**	Come mai Samanta **sonnecchia** a scuola?	**una dozzina** di uova	Non **trascinare** la borsa per terra!
809 down	810 to **doze**	811 dozen	812 to **drag**
il drago	**la libellula**	**lo scarico**	Roberto **disegna** bene.
813 dragon	814 dragonfly	815 drain/plug hole*	816 to **draw**

Alzate il **ponte levatoio!**

817 drawbridge

Le calze di Sabrina non sono in questo **cassetto.**

818 drawer

un bel **sogno**

819 a nice **dream**

Sta sognando delle pecore.

820 I **dream** of sheep.

il vestito

821 dress

vestirsi

822 to **dress**

Forse le calze di Sabrina sono in questo **cassettone.**

823 **dresser/chest of drawers***

sbavare

824 to **dribble**

Andare alla deriva non è molto divertente.

825 to **drift**

Patrizia **sta forando** una tavola.

826 to **drill**

il trapano electtrico

827 drill

una bevanda alcoolica

828 drink

gocciolare

830 to **drip**

Io **guido** con prudenza.

831 I **drive** carefully.

un guidatore imprudente

832 crazy **driver**

bere

829 to **drink**

pioggerella

La pioggerella è una pioggia leggera.

Drizzle is a light rain.

833 drizzle

Il Griso **sbava** alla vista del pollo.

834 to **drool**

una goccia di medicina

835 drop

L'ospite **ha lasciato cadere** il bicchiere.

836 to **drop**

Vieni a **farmi visita** in qualunque momento.

837   to **drop in**

Papà **lascia** il gatto dal veterinario.

838   Dad **drops off** the cat at the vet.

abbandonare la gara

839   to **drop out**

Sono assonnato.

840   I feel **drowsy**.

il tamburo

841   drum

una maglietta **asciutta**

842   dry

asciugare, far asciugare

843   to **dry**

una **lavanderia a secco**

844   dry cleaner

un essicatoio

845   dryer

la duchessa

846   duchess

un'anitra

847   duck

Un duello non è un bel modo di discutere.

848   duel

il duca

849   duke

il deposito dei rifiuti

850   dump

scaricare

851   to **dump**

un autocarro ribaltabile

852   dumptruck/lorry*

Il prigioniero è rinchiuso in **una cella sotterranea**.

853   dungeon

il crepuscolo

854   dusk

la polvere

855   dust

il nano

856   dwarf

Ciascun coniglio ha una carota.

857 **Each** rabbit has a carrot.

Le aquile sono animali rari e vanno protette.

858 eagle

un orecchio, un'orecchia

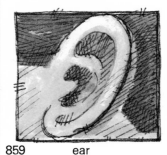

859 ear

Il sole sorge **presto**.

860 early

guadagnare, meritare

La mamma **guadagna** un buon salario.
Sabrina **si è meritata** una vacanza.

Mom earns a good wage.
Sabrina has earned a holiday.

861 to **earn**

il pianeta **Terra**

862 Earth

coltivare **la terra**

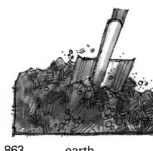

863 earth

il terremoto

864 earthquake

il cavalletto del pittore

865 easel

Est è dove sorge il sole.

866 east

Nuotare è **facile**.

867 Swimming is **easy**.

mangiare

868 to **eat**

fare colazione

869 to **eat** breakfast

fare pranzo

870 to **eat** lunch

fare cena

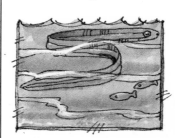

871 to **eat** dinner/supper*

L'eco rimanda la voce.

872 echo

un'eclisse di sole

873 eclipse

L'albero è sul **ciglio** del burrone.

874 The tree is at the **edge**.

un'anguilla

875 eel

La gallina ha fatto **un uovo**.	**una melanzana** di color violetto
876　egg	877　eggplant/aubergine*
otto insetti	**L'ottavo** pesce è rosso.
878　eight	879　eighth

Pippo gioca con **l'elastico**.
880　elastic

il gomito
881　elbow

le elezioni

Si tengono **le elezioni** per scegliere il governo.
Chi ha vinto **le elezioni**?

*Elections are held to choose the government.
Who won the election?*

882　election

un elettricista
883　electrician

l'elettricità
884　electricity

un elefante
885　elephant

un ascensore
886　elevator/lift*

l'alce
887　elk

un olmo
888　elm

Giorgio l'ha **imbarazzato**.
889　to embarrass

abbracciare
890　to embrace

il ricamo
891　embroidery

un'emergenza
892　emergency

La scatola è **vuota**.
893　The jar is **empty**.

E' **la fine** della strada.
894　This is the **end**.

Un giorno non saranno più **nemici**.
895　enemies

il motore di un'automobile

896   engine

il macchinista del treno

897   engineer/engine driver*

godere, godersi

898   to enjoy

I dinosauri erano animali **enormi.**

899   enormous dinosaur

abbastanza, basta

900   That is **enough.**

Fido **entra** dalla porta.

901   to enter

l'entrata

902   entrance

la busta

903   envelope

La loro forza è **uguale.**

904   equal

l'equatore

905   equator

la commissione

Sabrina sta facendo **una commissione** per suo papà. Ha molte **commissioni** da fare questa mattina.

Sabrina is running an errand for Dad.
She has many errands this morning.

906   errand

la scala mobile

907   escalator

Ce l'ha fatta a **scappare.**

908   to escape

L'Europa è un continente.

909   Europe

Il sole causa **l'evaporazione** dell'acqua.

910   evaporation

Quattro è un numero **pari.**

$n \times 2 = ?$

911   Four is an **even** number.

una superficie **piana**

912   an **even** surface

Il pino è una pianta **sempreverde.**

913   evergreen

ogni

Sabrina si fa il letto **ogni** mattina.
Devo dirtelo **ogni** volta?

Sabrina makes her bed every day.
Must I tell you every time?

914   every

un esame difficile

915   exam

esaminare con la lente

916   to examine

un esempio

Qualche volta Sabrina non dà buon **esempio**.
E' più facile capire quando si fa **un esempio**.

Sometimes Sabrina does not set a good example.
Things are easier to understand when you give an example.

917   example

il punto esclamativo

918   exclamation mark

Mi scusi!

919   Excuse me!

Giunone **fa ginnastica**.

920   to exercise

esistere

Esistere vuol dire essere.
I dinosauri non **esistono** più.

To exist is to be.
Dinosaurs no longer exist.

921   to exist

uscire

922   to exit/leave*

Il pallone **si dilata** finché scoppia.

923   to expand

aspettare, aspettarsi

Vi aspettiamo alle due.
Papà **si aspetta** che tu sia brava, Sabrina.

We expect you at two o'clock.
Dad expects you to be good, Sabrina.

924   to expect

caro, costoso

925   expensive

un esperimento

926   experiment

un'esperta

927   expert

Adesso te lo **spiego**.

928   to explain

L'avventuriero **esplora** la giungla.

929   to explore

un'esplosione

930   explosion

un estintore

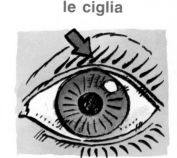

931   extinguisher

un occhio

932   eye

il sopracciglio

933   eyebrow

gli occhiali

934   eyeglasses/spectacles*

le ciglia

935   eyelash

la favola della cicala e della formica

936   fable

la faccia, **il viso**

937   face

la fabbrica

938   factory

Pierino **è stato bocciato**.

939   to fail

La macchina **si è rotta**.

940   to fail

la fiera

941   fair

La fata accoglierà un tuo desiderio.

942   fairy

fede, fiducia

Abbiamo **fiducia** in te.
Sabrina l'ha accettato **in buona fede**.

We have faith in you.
Sabrina accepted it in good faith.

943   faith

Questo quadro è **falso**.

944   fake painting

In **autunno** le foglie cadono.

945   fall/autumn*

cadere

946   to fall

Per fortuna, era un **falso allarme**.

949   false alarm

la famiglia

950   family

cadere, cascare

947   to fall down

cascare, fare una caduta

948   to fall off

Marilyn è un'attrice **famosa**.

951   famous actress

il ventilatore

952   fan

i costumi **eleganti**

953   fancy clothes

le zanne del leone

954   fang

La città è **lontana**.

955   The city is **far** away.

Addio!

956   Farewell !

Molti alimenti provengono dalle **fattorie**.

957   farm

il contadino, l'agricoltore

958   farmer

veloce

959   fast

allacciare la cintura di sicurezza

960   I **fasten** my seatbelt.

Brentano è **grasso** perché mangia troppi dolci.

961   fat

Il veleno è **mortale**.

962   fatal

il padre

963   father

Il rubinetto perde.

964   faucet/tap*

Di chi è **la colpa**?

965   Whose **fault** is it?

il favore

Posso chiederti **un favore**? Sabrina è gentile: fa volentieri **favori** alla gente.

Can I ask you a favor? Sabrina is nice; she likes doing people favors.

966   favor/favour*

Il mio gusto **preferito**!

967   favorite/favourite*

temere il peggio

968   to **fear** the worst

il banchetto

969   feast

E' **la piuma** di un canguro?

970   feather

Febbraio è il secondo mese dell'anno.

971   February

dar da mangiare

972   to feed

Mi sento bene.

973   I **feel** well.

La femmina dell'uccello fa le uova.

974   female

la staccionata

975   fence

il parafango

976   fender/wing*

la felce

977   fern

Meglio prendere il **traghetto** che nuotare!

978   ferry

la festa, **la celebrazione**

979   festival

Paolo ha **la febbre** alta.

980   fever

Pochi erano presenti.

981   **Few** people came.

il campo

982   field

Chiara è **la quinta**.

983   fifth

Questi sciocchi **bisticciano** sempre.

984   to **fight**

Fiorella si **lima** le unghie.

985   to **file**

riempire, **colmare**

986   to **fill**

una pellicola per la macchina fotografica

988   film

un maiale molto **sporco**

989   filthy

la pinna di uno squalo

990   fin

fare il pieno

987   to **fill up**

Il poliziotto le dà **una multa** per eccesso di velocità.

991   fine

Io **sto bene**.

992   I am **fine**.

il dito

993   finger

l'impronta digitale

994   fingerprint

Michele **ha terminato** la gara, arrivando primo.

995   to finish

Gli **abeti** hanno aghi.

996   fir

il fuoco

997   fire

la macchina dei pompieri

998   fire engine

l'uscita di sicurezza

999   fire escape

il petardo

1000   firecracker/banger*

il pompiere

1001   firefighter

il caminetto

1002   fireplace

la ditta, incrollabile

La ditta dello zio fabbrica giocattoli.
La decisione di papà è **incrollabile**: Pierino non può mangiare un altro gelato.

My uncle's firm makes toys. Dad's decision is firm: Pierino cannot have another ice cream.

1003   firm

il primo della fila

1004   first

il pesce

1005   fish

pescare

1006   to fish

un amo

1007   fishhook

il pugno

1008   fist

cinque

1009   five

Riuscirà a **riparare** la macchina?

1010   to fix

la bandiera dei pirati

1011   flag

I fiocchi di neve cadono dal cielo.

1012   flake

la fiamma

1013   flame

Cip-cip **batte** le ali.

1014   to flap

Un razzo può rischiarare la notte.	**il lampo** della macchina fotografica	**una lampada elettrica** portatile	**il matraccio**
1015 flare	1016 flash	1017 flashlight/torch*	1018 flask
piatto, liscio	**spianare**	Quale **gusto** preferisci?	**Baffo** ha **una pulce** sulla schiena.
1019 flat	1020 to flatten	1021 flavor/flavour*	1022 flea
fuggire	**il vello**	E' bene in **carne**.	**galleggiare**
1023 to flee	1024 fleece	1025 flesh	1026 to float
uno stormo d'uccelli	**un'inondazione**	**il pavimento**	Il fornaio fa il pane con **la farina**.
1027 flock	1028 flood	1029 floor	1030 flour
Il sangue **scorre**.	**il fiore**	Ugo ha preso **l'influenza**.	**il batuffolo, la lanugine**
1031 to flow	1032 flower	1033 flu	1034 fluff

L'acqua è un liquido.

1035　fluid

la mosca

1036　fly

la pattina dei pantaloni

1037　fly

Gli uccelli e gli aeroplani **volano.**

1038　to fly

la schiuma

1039　foam

La nebbia oscura la veduta.

1040　fog

Piegare seguendo le indicazioni.

1041　to fold

L'oca **segue** Battista ovunque.

1042　to follow

il cibo

1043　food

il piede

1044　foot

la palla da **football**

1045　American football

un'impronta nella neve

1046　footprint

Queste sono **le impronte** di Alberto.

1047　footsteps

per

Tutti **per** uno e uno **per** tutti.
Se non era **per** te, avremmo perso la partita.

One for all and all for one.
But for you, we would
have lost the game.

1048　for

forzare la porta

1049　to force

la fronte

1050　forehead

La foresta ospita molti animali.

1051　forest

dimenticare, scordarsi

Papà **si è dimenticato** di comprare il latte.
Il cane **ha dimenticato** il suo nome.
Scordatelo!

Dad forgot to buy milk.
Our dog has forgotten
his name.
Forget it!

1052　to **forget**

perdonare

Ti **perdono** se prometti di star buono.
Sabrina **ha perdonato** il cane che aveva mangiato la sua bambolina preferita.

I forgive you if you promise to be good.
Sabrina forgave her dog for eating her favorite doll.

1053　to **forgive**

la forchetta

1054　fork

un carrello sollevatore

1055 forklift

la figura

1056 form/tailor's dummy*

I soldati sono dentro **il forte**.

1057 fort

avanti

Avanti e indietro
Va **avanti** finché arrivi alla porta d'entrata.

Forward and backward
Go forward until you reach the front door.

1058 forward

Questo **fossile,** un tempo, era un pesce.

1059 fossil

un **cattivo** odore

1060 foul odor/odour*

le fondamenta di una casa

1061 foundation

la fontana

1062 fountain

La volpe è un animale astuto.

1063 fox

una frazione dell'intera torta

1064 fraction

Le uova sono molto **fragili**.

1065 fragile

la cornice

1066 frame

Hai **lentiggini** sul viso?

1067 freckle

Finalmente **libero**!

1068 free

Il suo succo d'arancia **è gelato.**

1069 to freeze

Frutta **fresca**, raccolta dall'albero.

1070 fresh

Il **venerdì** si mangia pesce.

Friday we eat fish.

1071 Friday

Il frigo, un altro nome per **frigorifero.**

1072 fridge

due **amici** per la pelle

1073 friends

Carla lo **ha spaventato**.

1074 to frighten

la rana

1075   frog

Io vengo **da** Marte.

1076   I am **from** Mars.

**il davanti,
la parte anteriore**

1077   front

Il gelo copre parte della finestra.

1078   frost

**acciglliarsi,
corrugare la fronte**

1079   to **frown**

La frutta è meglio dei dolciumi.

1080   fruit

friggere

1081   to **fry**

la padella

1082   frying pan

Le auto hanno bisogno di **carburante**.

1083   Cars need **fuel**.

pieno

1084   full

divertirsi

1085   having **fun**

la cassetta delle offerte

1086   charity **fund**

Un funerale è sempre triste.

1087   funeral

un imbuto

1088   funnel

divertente

Mamma non lo trova
divertente.
Ci è capitata una cosa
divertente mentre andavamo
a scuola.

*Mother does not think that is
funny.
A funny thing happened on
the way to school.*

1089   funny

Una pelliccia d'estate?

1090   fur coat

la caldaia del riscaldamento

1091   furnace/boiler*

i mobili

1092   furniture

La luce è mancata: sono saltati **i fusibili**.

1094   fuse

un gatto **dal pelo lungo**

1093   furry

un forte vento

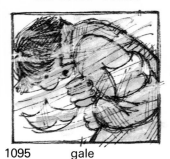

1095   gale

una galleria d'arte

1096   gallery

Un cavallo può trottare o **galoppare.**

1097   to gallop

il gioco delle palline

1098   game

Il papero è il maschio dell'oca.

1099   gander

una banda di delinquenti

1100   gang

Sabrina ha **uno spazio** tra gli incisivi.

1101   gap

L'auto si tiene nell'**autorimessa.**

1102   garage

i rifiuti, la spazzatura

1103   garbage/rubbish*

il bidone dell'immondizia

1104   garbage can/rubbish bin*

Le verdure si coltivano nell'**orto.**

1105   vegetable **garden**

fare gargarismi

1106   to gargle

L'aglio ha un odore pungente.

1107   garlic

la giarrettiera

1108   garter

il gas

Il pallone era pieno di **gas.**
Alcuni **gas** sono più leggeri dell'aria.
La mamma cucina su una stufa a **gas.**

*The balloon was filled with gas.
Some gases are lighter
than air.
Mom cooks on a gas stove.*

1109   gas

la benzina

1110   gas/petrol*

il pedale dell'**acceleratore**

1111   gas pedal/accelerator*

una pompa della benzina

1112   gas/petrol pump*

un distributore di benzina

1113   gas/petrol station*

il portone
1114 gate

Luciana **raccoglie** i fiori.
1115 to gather

gli ingranaggi
1116 gears

Il diamante è **una pietra preziosa**.
1117 gem

il generale
1118 general

un amico **generoso**
1119 a **generous** friend

una persona **gentile**
1120 a **gentle** person

Papà è un vero **gentiluomo**.
1121 gentleman

un **vero** porco
1122 a **genuine** pig

Tutti **studiano** la geografia.
1123 geography

il geranio
1124 geranium

il gerbillo
1125 gerbil

I germi causano malattie.
1126 germ

Fufi, **acchiappa** il topo!
1127 **Get** that mouse!

Voglio **averlo** indietro.
1128 I want to **get** it **back**.

entrare nella piscina
1129 to **get in** the pool

Sabrina **scende dall**'autobus.
1130 to **get off**

Sabrina **monta sull'** autobus.
1131 to **get on**

Si libera della spazzatura.
1132 to **get rid of**

Al mattino **si alza** presto.
1133 to **get up**

Hai paura dei **fantasmi**?
1134 ghost

il gigante
1135 giant

il regalo
1136 gift

una balena **gigantesca**
1137 gigantic

ridacchiare
1138 to giggle

Il pesce usa **le branchie** per respirare.
1139 gills

Lo **zenzero** è una spezia.
1140 ginger

un pane di zenzero
1141 gingerbread

una carovana di **gitani** in viaggio
1142 gipsy

La giraffa ha il collo lungo.
1143 giraffe

Adriana è **una ragazza**.
1144 girl

Pia **ha dato** l'ombrello ad Anna.
1145 to give

il ghiacciaio
1148 glacier

Sono **contento**.
1149 I am glad.

un pannello di **vetro**
1150 glass

Anna glielo **ha restituito** quando è tornato il sole.
1146 to give back

Porti **gli occhiali**?
1152 glasses

scivolare
1153 to glide

un bicchiere d'acqua
1151 glass

Mi arrendo!
1147 I give up!

Un aliante è un aereo senza motore.

1154   glider

i guanti

1155   gloves

la colla

1156   glue

andare, partire

1157   to **go**

Il portiere difende **la porta**.

1161   goal

la capra

1162   goat

occhiali di protezione

1163   goggles

L'operaio **scende** a lavorare.

1158   to **go down**

---

il lingotto **d'oro**

1164   gold

il pesciolino rosso

1165   goldfish

Zio Gianni gioca a **golf**.

1166   golf

Fido **entra** nella cuccia per fare un pisolino.

1159   to **go in**

Ha un **buon** sapore.

1167   good

Ciao, mamma.

1168   Goodbye!

un'oca

1169   goose

Jack **sale** sulla pianta di fagioli.

1160   to **go up**

---

l'uva spina

1170   gooseberry

Lei pensa d'avere una pettinatura **stupenda**.

1171   gorgeous

il gorilla

1172   gorilla

governare

Il governo **governa** la nazione.
Governare una nazione non è così facile come sembra.

The government governs the country.
It is not as easy to govern a country as it seems.

1173   to **govern**

il governo

Il governo è eletto dalla popolazione.
Il papà di Sabrina, che è ammiraglio, lavora per **il governo**.

The government is elected by the people.
Sabrina's dad, the admiral, works for the government.

1174   government

Sarà punito per aver **afferrato** il gelato di Pia.

1175   to grab

E' molto **compito**.

1176   He is very **gracious.**

Frequento la prima **classe.**

1177   grade / form*

Raccogliamo **il grano** per ottenerne farina.

1178   grain

1000 **grammi** = 1 chilogrammo

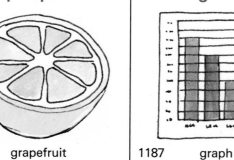

1179   gram

---

i nonni e il loro **nipote**

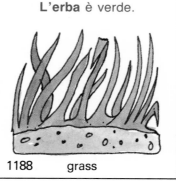

1180   grandchild

---

il nonno

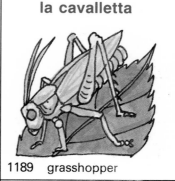

1181   grandfather

Alla nonna di Sabrina piace cucinare.

1182   grandmother

Il granito è una pietra dura.

1183   granite

---

concedere, esaudire

Ti **concedo** una licenza di dieci giorni.
La buona fata **esaudirà** tre dei tuoi desideri.

I grant you ten days' leave of absence.
The good fairy will grant you three wishes.

1184   to grant

---

un grappolo d'**uva**

1185   grapes

---

il pompelmo

1186   grapefruit

---

il grafico

1187   graph

L'erba è verde.

1188   grass

---

la cavalletta

1189   grasshopper

---

la grattugia

1190   grater

---

la tomba

1191   grave

---

la ghiaia lungo la strada

1192   gravel

La gravità fa cadere la mela.

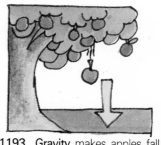

1193   **Gravity** makes apples fall.

Le mucche **pascolano** nel prato.

1194   to **graze**

Il grasso porrà fine allo scricchiolio.

1195   **grease**

un **magnifico** giocattolo

1196   a **great** toy

avido

1197   **greedy**

Verde è il colore dell'erba.

1198   **green**

i fagiolini verdi

1199   **green** bean

la serra

1200   **greenhouse**

Giovanni **saluta** sempre le signore.

1201   to **greet**

Di notte tutti i gatti sono **grigi**.

1202   **grey*/gray**

cuocere ai ferri

1203   to **grill**

sporco, sudicio

1204   **grimy**

Gianmarco **sorride** felice.

1205   to **grin**

Il macellaio **macina** la carne.

1206   to **grind**/to **mince***

Sara **stringe** con forza le manopole.

1207   to **grip**

gemere, lamentarsi

1208   to **groan**

Il droghiere accoglie una cliente.

1209   **grocer**

lo sposo e la sposa

1211   **groom**

Lo stalliere si prende cura dei cavalli.

1212   **groom**

Patrizia **si fa bella**.

1213   to **groom**

Piero compera **le provviste**.

1210   shopping for **groceries**

la scanalatura

1214 groove

Questo essere è **disgustoso.**

1215 gross/disgusting*

il terreno

1216 ground

la marmotta

1217 groundhog

un gruppo di persone

1218 group

crescere

1219 to grow

ringhiare

1220 to growl

un adulto

1221 grown-up

fare la guardia

1222 to guard

Aspetta! Lasciami **indovinare.**

1223 to guess

Il monaco accoglie **l'ospite.**

1224 guest

Lo **conduce** nella sua stanza.

1225 to guide

colpevole

Sabrina dice che non è **colpevole.**
E' **colpevole** colui che ha preso il barattolo delle caramelle.

Sabrina says she is not guilty. Whoever took the candy jar is guilty.

1226 guilty

un porcellino d'India, una cavia

1227 guinea pig

Pablo suona **la chitarra.**

1228 guitar

il **Golfo** del Messico

1229 Gulf of Mexico

I gabbiani vivono vicino all'acqua.

1230 gull

Le gengive coprono le radici dei denti.

1231 gum

Masticare **gomma** non è proprio la miglior abitudine.

1232 gum/chewing gum*

L'acqua scola nella **cunetta.**

1233 gutter

Fumare è **una** cattiva **abitudine**.	**un aglefino**	una tempesta di **grandine**	
1234 bad **habit**	1235 haddock	1236 hail	
La sorella di Sabrina ha tantissimi **capelli**.	**la spazzola per capelli**	**il parrucchiere**	Che grosso **asciugacapelli**!
1237 hair	1238 hairbrush	1239 hairdresser	1240 hairdryer
Vuoi l'altra **metà**?	**l'entrata, l'atrio**	**L'Halloween** è la notte delle streghe.	**il corridoio**
1241 half	1242 hall	1243 Halloween/Hallowe'en*	1244 hallway/corridor*
Il soldato **si fermò** fuori dalla porta.	**il martello**	**martellare** un pezzo di legno	**l'amaca**
1245 to halt	1246 hammer	1247 to hammer	1248 hammock
il criceto	**Una mano** ha cinque dita.	**dar via, distribuire**	**il freno a mano**
1249 hamster	1250 hand	1251 to hand out	1252 hand brake

le manette

1253   handcuffs

handicap, svantaggio

Essere ciechi è un **handicap,** ma si può superare qualsisi **svantaggio.**

Being blind is a handicap, but people can overcome any handicap.

1254   handicap

la maniglia

1255   handle

il corrimano

1256   handrail

Maurizio è convinto d'essere **bello.**

1257   handsome

una persona **capace** di fare di tutto

1258   handy person

Appendere il quadro diritto.

1259   to hang

tenere duro

1260   to hang on

---

aviorimessa

1262   hangar

Appendi il cappotto sull' **appendiabiti.**

1263   hanger

il fazzoletto da naso

1264   handkerchief

appendere una maglietta

1261   to hang up

Gli incidenti possono **capitare.**

1265   Accidents happen.

Lui è **felice.**

1266   He is happy.

Le barche sono nel **porto.**

1267   harbor/harbour*

Troppo **duri** da rompere.

1268   hard

---

la lepre

1269   hare

Non si deve **fare del male** agli animali!

1270   to harm

un'armonica

1271   harmonica

La briglia fa parte dei **finimenti** del cavallo.

1272   harness

un'arpa	un inverno **rigido**	Giuseppe **miete** il grano.	**il cappello**
1273 harp	1274 a **harsh** winter	1275 to harvest	1276 hat
E' bello veder **schiudere** i pulcini.	**un'accetta**	Il pirata **trasporta** un sacco pesante.	una casa **infestata dagli spettri**
1277 to **hatch**	1278 hatchet	1279 to **haul**	1280 **haunted** house
Maria **ha** la bambola che Gina vuole.	**Il falco** è un uccello da preda.	**il fieno** per i cavalli	**La foschia** rende le figure indistinte.
1281 to **have**	1282 hawk	1283 hay	1284 **Haze** makes for a hazy day.
il nocciolo	**La nocciola** è il frutto del nocciolo.	**la testa**	Ho **mal di testa**.
1285 hazel	1286 hazelnut	1287 head	1288 I have a **headache**.
il poggiacapo	La gamba rotta sta **guarendo**.	un fiore **sano**	**un mucchio** di spazzatura
1289 headrest	1290 to **heal**	1291 **healthy** flower	1292 heap/pile*

sento una voce

1293   I **hear** a voice.

Il cuore batte nel petto.

1294   heart

scaldare, riscaldare

1295   to **heat**

il radiatore, il calorifero

1296   heater/radiator*

sollevare

1297   to **heave**

il paradiso

1298   heaven

un elefante **pesante**

1299   one **heavy** elephant

Hai potato **la siepe**?

1300   hedge

L'istrice ha aculei sulla schiena.

1301   hedgehog

il calcagno

1302   heel

un elicottero

1303   helicopter

l'inferno

1304   hell

Salve !

1305   hello

il timone, la ruota del timone

1306   helm

Il soldato porta **l'elmetto**.

1307   helmet

La mamma di Sabrina **aiuta** un automobilista.

1308   to help

Un neonato è **inerme**.

1309   helpless

l'orlatura, il bordo

1310   hem

Il globo terrestre ha due **emisferi**.

1311   hemisphere

la gallina

1312   hen

Un ettagono ha sette lati.

1313   heptagon

le erbe

1314   herbs

una mandria di buoi

1315   herd

Vieni **qui!**

1316   Come **here!**

L'eremita vive da solo.

1317   hermit

un eroe

1318   hero

un'eroina

1319   heroine

un'aringa

1320   herring

Paolo **esita** a tuffarsi.

1321   to **hesitate**

Un esagono ha sei lati.

1322   hexagon

Gli orsi **vanno in letargo** d'inverno.

1323   to **hibernate**

avere il singhiozzo

1324   to **hiccup/hiccough***

Il cuoio è la pelle di un animale.

1325   hide

Olga **si nasconde.**

1326   to **hide**

il nascondiglio

1327   hiding-place

una montagna molto **alta**

1328   a **high** mountain

un edificio alto

1329   highrise/tower block*

una scuola secondaria

1330   high school/secondary school*

una strada maestra, un'autostrada

1331   highway/motorway*

sequestrare un aereo

1332   to **hijack** a plane

Una collina con un albero in cima.

1333   hill

la cerniera

1334   hinge

le gambe **posteriori**

1335   hind legs

la mano sull'**anca**

1336   hand on **hip**

un ippopotamo

1337   hippopotamus

Studio **la storia**.

1338   I study **history**.

battere, colpire

1339   to **hit**

Le api vivono in **un alveare**.

1340   hive

accaparrare

1341   to **hoard**

una voce **roca**

1342   **hoarse** voice

Lavorare a maglia è **un passatempo** per la mamma.

1343   hobby

Mio fratello gioca a **hockey**.

1344   hockey/ice hockey*

la zappa

1347   hoe

Sabrina **tiene stretto** Tigre, il gatto.

1348   to **hold**

Sabrina non dovrebbe **tenerlo giù a terra**.

1349   to **hold down**

un dischetto da hockey

1345   hockey puck

il buco

1350   hole

Zio Dario ha lavorato sodo per andare in **vacanza**.

1351   holiday

Gli scoiattoli abitano in questo albero **cavo**.

1352   **hollow** tree

un bastone da hockey

1346   hockey stick

l'agrifoglio con le sue bacche rosse

1353   holly

In India, la vacca è un animale **sacro.**

1354   a **holy** cow

Gli scoiattoli sono **a casa.**

1355   home

Luca fa **il compito.**

1356   homework

E' **onesto** quel tale?

1357   Is he **honest?**

Gli orsi sono ghiotti di **miele.**

1358   honey

il favo di miele

1359   honeycomb

il melone verde

1360   honeydew melon

suonare il clacson

1361   to **honk**

Che **onore,** ricevere un diploma!

1362   honor/honour*

Il mantello di Sabrina ha **il cappuccio.**

1363   hood

Il motore è nel **cofano.**

1364   hood/bonnet*

lo zoccolo del cavallo

1365   hoof

l'amo

1366   hook

Baffo salta attraverso **il cerchio.**

1367   jump through a **hoop**

saltare, saltellare

1368   to **hop**

Spero di vincere.

1369   I **hope** to win.

E' un caso **disperato:** non imparerà mai a cavalcare.

1370   hopeless

il gioco della settimana

1371   hopscotch/hop-scotch*

Il sole sorge all' **orizzonte.**

1372   horizon

in posizione **orizzontale**	la **tromba**, il **clacson**	il **corno inglese**	il **corno**
1373 horizontal	1374 horn	1375 French **horn**	1376 horn
Il **calabrone** punge col suo pungiglione.	il **cavallo**	il **rafano**	un **ferro di cavallo**
1377 hornet	1378 horse	1379 horseradish	1380 horseshoe
un **tubo di gomma**	un **ospedale**	Fa veramente **caldo**.	E' talmente **piccante** che mi brucia la lingua.
1381 hose	1382 hospital	1383 hot	1384 hot
Quando viaggiamo, stiamo in **albergo**.	Vi sono 60 minuti in **un'ora**.	la **clessidra**	il **peperoncino** piccante
1386 hotel	1387 hour	1388 hourglass	1385 hot pepper
la **casa**	uno **hovercraft**	Ti insegno **come** fare.	Il cane **ulula** nella notte.
1389 house	1390 hovercraft	1391 I will show you **how**.	1392 to howl

il coprimozzo

1393   hub cap

il mirtillo

1394   huckleberry

stringersi insieme, accalcarsi

1395   to huddle

L'elefante è **enorme**.

1396   huge

lo scafo della nave

1397   hull

il colibrì

1398   hummingbird

Il cammello ha due **gobbe**.

1399   hump

cento

1400   hundred

Ella **ha fame**.

1401   She is **hungry**.

Mirone **caccia** con un fucile.

1402   to **hunt**

lanciare, scagliare

1403   to hurl

Chi dà il nome agli **uragani?**

1404   hurricane

affrettarsi

1405   to hurry

Il polso mi **fa male**.

1406   My wrist **hurts**.

Edoardo è **il marito** di Paola.

1407   husband

la capanna

1408   hut

la credenza, il buffet

1409   hutch/sideboard*

il giacinto

1410   hyacinth

Il coro canta **un inno**.

1411   hymn

il trattino

Il trattino si trova nelle parole composte. Uomo-lupo è una parola composta e contiene **un trattino.**

Compound words contain a hyphen. In Italian, wherewolf is a compound word and has a hyphen.

1412   hyphen

Il ghiaccio galleggia nel bicchiere.

1413   ice

il gelato

1414   ice cream

Gli **iceberg** possono far affondare le navi.

1415   iceberg

I ghiaccioli pendono dal tetto.

1416   icicle

La torta viene decorata con **zucchero a velo**.

1417   icing

Ha avuto **un'idea** luminosa.

1418   idea

due gemelli **identici**

1419   identical twins

un idiota

1420   idiot

ozioso, pigro

1421   idle

se

Se avessi un martello, lo userei solo quando nessuno dorme.
Te lo comprerei, **se** potessi.

*If I had a hammer, I would only hammer when no one is sleeping.
I would buy it for you if I could.*

1422   if

un iglù

1423   igloo

la chiave dell'accensione

1424   ignition key

Paolo è **malato** da vari giorni.

1425   ill

illuminare

1426   to illuminate

una illustrazione

Le figure nei libri si chiamano **illustrazioni**.
Questo libro ha molte **illustrazioni**.

*Pictures in books are called illustrations.
This dictionary has many illustrations.*

1427   illustration

importante

Quel che è **importante** per Sabrina, non è forse molto **importante** per Luca.
Leggere e scrivere sono cose **importanti**.

*What is important to Sabrina may not be important to Luca.
Reading and writing are important matters.*

1428   important

in, nel (nella, nelle, negli)

La famiglia Rossi sta progettando un picnic **nel** parco.
Porteranno anche Baffo **in** macchina con loro.

*The Rossi family is planning a picnic in the park.
They will take Baffo along in the car.*

1429   in

L'incenso si brucia in chiesa.

1430   incense

Per fare un piede ci vogliono dodici **pollici**.

1431   inch

indice

C'è **un indice** alla fine di questo libro.
L'indice contiene tutte le parole del dizionario.

There is an index at the back of this book.
The index contains all the words in this dictionary.

1432   index

il color **indaco**

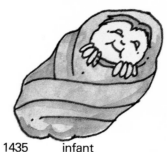

1433   indigo

all'interno

1434   indoors

il neonato, il bebè

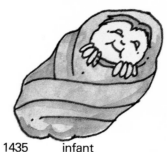

1435   infant

Zia Silvia ha **un'infezione**.

1436   infection

infettivo, contagioso

La sua malattia è **infettiva**.
La risata di papà è **contagiosa**.

Her condition is infectious.
Dad has an infectious laugh.

1437   infectious

Anna **informa** Lucia che traslocherà.

1438   to inform

L'orso **abita** nella caverna.

1439   The bear **inhabits** a cave.

---

le iniziali

1440   initials

un'iniezione nel braccio

1441   injection

una ferita al dito

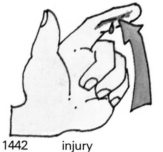

1442   injury

L'inchiostro è nel calamaio.

1443   ink

Vi sono molti tipi di **insetti**.

1444   insect

dentro la scatola

1445   inside

Insisto che tu faccia il bagno!

1446   to insist

ispezionare, esaminare

1447   to inspect

Usa un cucchiaio **invece di** una forchetta.

1449   Use a spoon **instead of** a fork!

le istruzioni per l'uso

1450   instruction

un istruttore

1451   instructor

un ispettore

1448   inspector

l'isolamento, il materiale isolante

L'isolamento dei fili elettrici serve a prevenire le scosse elettriche.
C'è **materiale isolante** nei muri della casa.

The insulation of electric wires prevents shocks.
There is insulation in the walls of the house.

1452   insulation

un incrocio

1453   intersection/crossroads*

un'intervista, il colloquio

1454   interview

Daniele entra **nella** stanza.

1455   into the room

Mamma **presenta** Dino a Fausto.

1456   to introduce

I Vichingi **invasero** altre nazioni.

1457   to invade

Alcuni divennero **invalidi.**

1458   invalid

Non ricordo di aver **inventato** quest'albero!

1459   to invent

un uomo **invisibile**

1460   invisible

Ha ricevuto **un invito** alla nostra festa.

1461   invitation

E' lui che l'**ha invitata.**

1462   He is inviting her.

un giaggiolo, un iris

1463   iris

Antonio si **stira** i pantaloni.

1464   to iron

il ferro da stiro

1465   iron

la maschera di **ferro**

1466   iron mask

un'isola

1467   island

il prurito

Roberto ha **un** forte **prurito,** causato dall'edera del Canada.
Il prurito passerà, se lui non si gratta.

Roberto has a bad itch from poison ivy.
The itch will go away if he does not scratch.

1468   itch

avere il prurito

1469   to itch

La pelle mi **prude.**

1470   My skin is itchy.

L'edera si arrampica sui muri.

1471   ivy

colpire con un diretto sinistro
1472　to jab

La giacca non è della misura giusta.
1473　jacket

la sopraccoperta di un libro
1474　dust jacket

un bordo **frastagliato**
1475　jagged edge

dietro le sbarre della **prigione**
1476　jail/gaol*

la marmellata
1477　jam

bloccare la porta
1478　to jam

Gennaio è il primo mese dell'anno.
1479　January

il vasetto
1480　jar

Questo squalo ha **fauci** spaventose!
1481　jaw

i jeans
1482　jeans

la jeep, la camionetta
1483　jeep

la gelatina di frutta
1484　jelly

un motore **a reazione**
1485　jet engine

un aereo **a reazione**
1486　jet plane

il gioiello
1488　jewel

il gioco delle composizioni
1489　jigsaw puzzle

fare **un lavoro**
1490　doing a job

il getto d'acqua
1487　jet of water

Il fantino monta un cavallo da corsa.

1491   jockey

correre

1492   to jog

congiungere le due parti

1493   to join

l'articolazione del gomito

1494   joint

Zio Pierino pensa che sia proprio **un** bello **scherzo!**

1495   joke

Il giudice deciderà.

1496   judge

il giocoliere

1497   juggler

A Nina piace **il succo** d'arancia fresco.

1498   juice

Luglio è un buon mese per nuotare.

1499   July

La rana **salta**.

1500   to jump

Essa **salta dentro** l'acqua...

1501   to jump in

...poi **salta sopra** una pietra.

1502   to jump on

Antonio è un buon **saltatore**.

1503   jumper

lo scamiciato

1504   jumper/pinafore*

i cavi d'emergenza

1505   jumper cables/jump leads*

Giugno è un buon mese per il tennis.

1506   June

Ci sono tigri nella **giungla**.

1507   jungle

La giunca è una barca cinese.

1508   junk

i rottami, **i rifiuti**

1509   junk

appena, giusto

Sabrina è **appena** arrivata a casa.
Il giudice è **giusto**.

Sabrina just got home.
The judge is a just person.

1510   just

K

il caleidoscopio
1511   kaleidoscope

il canguro
1512   kangaroo

la chiglia di una barca a vela
1513   keel

Fido è contento del suo **canile.**
1514   kennel

un chicco di granturco
1515   kernel

il bollitore
1516   kettle

la chiave
1517   key

calciare
1518   to kick

il ragazzino
1519   kid

Anche le capre hanno dei **piccoli.**
1520   kid

Solo i criminali **sequestrano** le persone.
1521   to kidnap

un rene
1522   kidney

Il cacciatore **ha ucciso** il leone.
1523   to kill

I vasi d'argilla cuociono nel **forno.**
1524   kiln

1 chilogrammo = 1000 grammi
1525   kilogram

1 chilometro = 1000 metri
1526   kilometer/kilometre*

il kilt, il gonnellino scozzese
1527   kilt

Il vestito è **una specie** di indumento.
1528   A dress is a **kind** of garment.

una bambina **gentile**
1529   **kind** girl

Il re porta la corona.

1530   king

il martin pescatore

1531   kingfisher

l'edicola dei giornali

1532   kiosk

un'aringa affumicata

1533   kippers

baciare

1534   to kiss

Dammi **un bacio**.

1535   kiss

la cucina

1536   kitchen

L'aquilone vola alto nel cielo.

1537   kite

Il micino diventerà un gatto.

1538   kitten

il kiwi

1539   kiwi

il ginocchio

1540   knee

inginocchiarsi

1541   to kneel

il coltello

1542   knife

Sai **lavorare a maglia**?

1543   to knit

la maniglia della porta

1544   knob

bussare alla porta

1545   to knock

il nodo

1546   knot

sapere, conoscere

Sai che cosa significa?
Sabrina **sa** il francese.
Conosco quell'uomo.

Do you know what it means?
Sabrina knows French.
I know that man.

1547   to know

la nocca, l'articolazione

1548   knuckle

Il koala vive in Australia.

1549   koala bear

L

L'etichetta avverte del pericolo.

1550　　label

il laboratorio

1551　　laboratory

un colletto di **trine**

1552　　lace

la scala

1554　　ladder

il mestolo

1555　　ladle

la signora

1556　　lady

Marco **si allaccia** le scarpe.

1553　　to lace

la coccinella

1557　　ladybug/ladybird*

le lingue di gatto

1558　　ladyfingers

Il mostro è nella sua **tana**.

1559　　lair

Il lago è circondato dalla terra.

1560　　lake

un agnello

1561　　lamb

L'asino è **zoppo**.

1562　　lame

la lampada

1563　　lamp

un lampione

1564　　lamp-post

la lancia del fante

1565　　lance

la terra

1566　　land

L'aereo **atterra**.

1567　　to land

il pianerottolo

1568　　landing

il padrone di casa

L'appartamento in cui viviamo appartiene al nostro **padrone di casa**. Ogni mese noi paghiamo l'affitto al **padrone di casa**.

The apartment in which we live belongs to the landlord. Every month we pay rent to the landlord.

1569　landlord

Le autostrade hanno parecchie **corsie**.

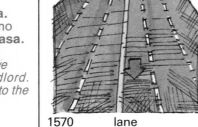

1570　lane

---

la lingua

Quante **lingue** parli? L'italiano è **la lingua** materna di Sabrina.

How many languages can you speak?
Italian is Sabrina's first language.

1571　language

---

la lanterna

1572　lantern

La balia tiene il bimbo in **grembo**.

1573　lap

---

il larice

1574　larch

Il lardo fonde nella padella.

1575　lard

---

grande, grosso

1576　large

---

un'allodola

1577　lark

---

le ciglia

1578　lash

---

l'**ultimo** pezzo

1579　the **last** piece

Certe cose **durano** a lungo.

1580　Some things do **last**.

Metti il chiavistello, per favore!

1581　to **latch**

Sei **in ritardo**.

1582　You are **late**.

---

la schiuma di sapone, la saponata

1583　lather

---

ridere

1584　to laugh

La scialuppa li porta a riva.

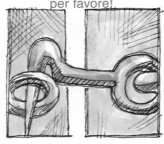

1585　launch

---

lanciare un missile

1586　to launch

---

la piattaforma di lancio

1587　launchpad

---

i panni sporchi

1588　laundry/washing*

Carmela fa **il bucato** in lavanderia.
1589   laundry/launderette*

La lavanda ha un buon profumo.
1590   lavender

Osserva **la legge**!
1591   Obey the law!

Chi ha tagliato l'erba del **prato**?
1592   lawn

posare le piastrelle
1594   to lay tiles

uno strato sopra l'altro
1595   layer upon layer

E' molto **pigro**.
1596   He is lazy.

falciatrice per tappeti erbosi
1593   lawn mower

Vincenzo **conduce** il cavallo.
1597   to lead

il capo del gruppo
1598   leader

la foglia
1599   leaf

Il secchio **perde**.
1600   to leak

La Torre di Pisa **pende**.
1601   to lean

Sto imparando a leggere.
1602   I learn to read.

il guinzaglio di Bobi
1603   leash/lead*

Le scarpe sono fatte di **pelle**.
1604   Shoes are made of leather.

Lascio il pacco alla porta.
1605   to leave

Antonio sta **partendo.**
1606   to leave

il davanzale della finestra
1607   ledge of a window

il porro
1608   leek

Gira a **sinistra**!	E' **mancino**.	**la gamba**	**la leggenda** del ciclope
1609 left	1610 He is **left-handed**.	1611 leg	1612 legend
il limone	**la limonata**	Ti posso **prestare** questo libro.	**la lente** degli occhiali
1613 lemon	1614 lemonade	1615 to **lend**	1616 lens
Il **leopardo** sta in agguato.	**la calzamaglia**	Ce ne sono **di meno** in questa pila.	**la lezione** del saggio
1617 leopard	1618 leotard	1619 There is **less** here.	1620 lesson
Lasciami andare!	**una lettera** dell'alfabeto M	Sabrina ha scritto **una lettera**.	**La lattuga** cresce nell'orto.
1621 **Let** me go!	1622 letter of the alphabet	1623 letter	1624 lettuce
una superficie **piana**	**la leva**	Il **bugiardo** è stato punito.	In **biblioteca** si fa silenzio.
1625 level surface	1626 lever	1627 liar	1628 library

la targa dell'automobile

1629   licence plate/number plate*

leccare

1630   to lick

il coperchio del barattolo

1631   lid

Pinocchio sta **dicendo una bugia**.

1632   to lie

La vita del bimbo è cominciata.

1634   life

la scialuppa di salvataggio

1635   lifeboat

sollevare

1636   to lift

coricarsi

1633   to lie down

La lampada fa **luce**.

1637   light/table lamp*

Papà **accende** la candela.

1638   to light

la lampadina

1639   lightbulb

Gli **alleggerisce** il carico.

1640   She **lightens** the load.

il faro

1641   lighthouse

il lampo

1642   lightning

il parafulmine

1643   lightning rod

A Sara **piace** il gatto nero.

1644   to like

probabilmente, verosimile

Franca **probabilmente** non verrà domani.
E' una storia **verosimile**.

Franca is not likely to come tomorrow.
It is a likely story!

1645   likely

I lillà fioriscono in primavera.

1646   lilac

il giglio

1647   lily

il ramo di un albero

1648   limb

il cedro

1649   lime

il limite

Il limite di velocità è di 50 chilometri all'ora.
La gentilezza della mamma non ha **limite**.

The speed limit is 50 kilometers per hour.
Mom's kindness has no limit.

1650   limit

Il nostro vicino **zoppica**.

1651   to limp

la linea

Sei capace di tracciare **una linea** veramente diritta?

1652   line

La biancheria è nell'armadio.

1653   linen

Il transatlantico naviga nell'oceano.

1654   liner

la fodera della giacchetta

1655   lining

collegare, unire

1656   to link

la lanuggine

1657   lint

il leone

1658   lion

le labbra

1659   lips

il rossetto per le labbra

1660   lipstick

L'acqua è **un liquido**.

1661   liquid

la lista

1662   list

Essi **ascoltano**.

1663   They are **listening**.

il litro

1664   liter/litre*

Non **gettare** mai **i rifiuti per terra**.

1665   to litter

una **piccola** mela

1666   a little apple

abitare, vivere

Sabrina **abita** in città.
La zia Filomena **è vissuta** 90 anni.

Sabrina lives in the city.
Aunt Filomena lived ninety years.

1667   to live

vivace

1668   lively

il salotto

1669　living room/lounge*

la lucertola

1670　lizard

Il soldato **carica** il cannone.

1671　'to load

caricare un autocarro

1672　to load

la pagnotta

1673　loaf

prestare

Enzo ha prestato dei soldi a Sabrina perché lei ha speso tutta la sua paghetta.

Enzo loaned Sabrina some money because she had spent all her allowance.

1674　to loan/lend*

un'aragosta

1675　lobster

mettere la sicura, chiudere a chiave

1676　to lock

la locomotiva

1678　locomotive

la cavalletta

1679　locust

un casotto per la caccia

1680　lodge/chalet*

la serratura

1677　lock

Il solaio è sotto il tetto.

1681　loft

il tronco

1682　log

il lecca-lecca

1683　lollipop

solo, solitario

1684　lonely

La giraffa ha il collo **lungo**.

1685　long

guardare la vetrina

1686　to look

il telaio per la tessitura

1687　loom

il cappio

1688　loop

Il braccialetto è troppo **allentato.**

1689   loose

Bruno **ha perso** una manopola.

1690   to **lose**

la lozione per la pelle

1691   lotion

La musica è troppo **forte.**

1692   loud

il megafono

1693   loudspeaker

oziare, poltrire

1694   to **lounge**

l'amore

L'amore è una cosa molto importante.
Sabrina dice che quando si ha **l'amore**, si ha tutto.

Love is very important.
Sabrina says that if you have love you have everything.

1695   love

Si amano.

1696   to **love**

graziosa, attraente

1697   lovely

un ramo **basso**

1698   **low** branch

abbassare, calare

1699   to **lower**

fortunato

Luca è stato **fortunato** perché è andato al campeggio.
Sabrina è **fortunata** ad avere un fratello così simpatico.

Luca was very lucky to be sent to camp.
Sabrina is lucky to have such a cute brother.

1700   lucky

i bagagli

1701   luggage

L'acqua **tiepida** non è né calda, né fredda.

1702   **lukewarm** water

Mamma canta **la ninna nanna** al suo bambino.

1703   lullaby

il legname da costruzione

1704   lumber/timber*

il gonfiore, il bernoccolo

1705   lump

la seconda colazione

1706   lunch

il cestino della colazione

1707   lunchbox

E' importante avere **i polmoni** sani.

1708   lung

M

la rivista illustrata

1709   magazine

Le larve non sono molto belle.

1710   maggot

una strana **magia** ...

1711   magic

La calamita attira i chiodi.

1713   magnet

un **magnifico** leone

1714   magnificent

La lente ingrandisce l'insetto.

1715   magnifying glass

Il mago fa comparire un coniglietto.

1712   magician

la gazza

1716   magpie

spedire per posta, imbucare

1717   to mail/post*

Il postino consegna la posta.

1718 mail carrier/postman*

Che cosa **fa** Marco?

1719   to make

il trucco di Milena

1720   makeup

il maschio e la femmina

1721   male

il maglio, il mazzuolo

1722   mallet

un uomo

1723   man

Il mandarino è un frutto delizioso.

1724   mandarin

Suona **il mandolino**.

1725   mandolin

la criniera del cavallo

1726   mane

Il mango è un frutto dolcissimo.

1727   mango

Conosce le buone **maniere**.
1728 He has good **manners**.

molte pesche
1729 many

la mappa, la carta geografica
1730 map

Lo scultore lavora **il marmo**.
1731 marble

marciare
1733 to march

Marzo è il terzo mese dell'anno.
1734 March

la cavalla, la giumenta
1735 mare

le palline
1732 marbles

la calendola
1736 marigold

segnare la risposta giusta
1737 to mark

Hai preso **un** bel **voto**.
1738 mark

il mercato della frutta e verdura
1739 market

sposarsi
1740 to marry

la palude
1741 marsh

schiacciare le patate, fare la purè
1742 to **mash** potatoes

la maschera
1743 mask

la massa
1744 mass

l'albero della barca a vela
1745 mast

Lucia **conosce bene** le regole della circolazione.
1746 to master

un incontro, una gara di tennis
1747 match

Non bisogna giocare con **i fiammiferi**.

1748 match

la matematica

1749 mathematics

la cosa, **la faccenda**

Copiare a scuola è **una cosa** grave.
Questa è **una faccenda** che non capisco.

To cheat in school is a serious matter.
This is a matter I do not understand.

1750 matter

Il materasso è vecchio.

1751 mattress

Maggio è il quinto mese dell'anno.

1752 May

forse

Forse Sabrina dovrebbe restare a casa.
La risposta non è né sì né no: è **forse**.

Maybe Sabrina should stay home.
The answer is not yes, and it is not no: it is maybe.

1753 maybe

il sindaco della città

1754 mayor

Non perderti nel **labirinto**!

1755 maze

il prato

1756 meadow

lo stornello americano

1757 meadowlark

il pasto

1758 meal

un ragazzo **cattivo**

1759 mean person

Marianna ha **il morbillo**.

1760 measles

misurare

1761 to measure

la carne

1762 meat

il meccanico

1763 mechanic

Sara ha vinto **una medaglia** per il suo coraggio.

1764 medal

Una medicina prescritta dal dottore.

1765 medicine

medio

1766 medium

incontrare

1767 to meet

la riunione degli insegnanti

1768   meeting

il melone

1769   melon

fondere, sciogliersi

1770   to melt

Il nostro club ha quattro **membri**.

1771   Our club has four members.

il menu del ristorante

1772   menu

mercè, pietà

Siamo alla **mercè** del tempo.
I banditi non hanno avuto nessuna **pietà**.

We are at the mercy of the weather.
The bandits showed no mercy.

1773   mercy

la sirena

1774   mermaid

allegro, giocondo

1775   merry

un disordine terribile

1776   a real mess

C'è **un messaggio** per te.

1777   message

il messaggero

1778   messenger

un boccale di **metallo**

1779   metal

Le meteoriti provengono dallo spazio.

1780   meteorite

il contatore

1781   meter

Un metro contiene cento centimetri.

1782   meter/metre*

il metodo

Sabrina ha **un metodo** per imparare rapidamente.
Un metodo è un modo di fare le cose.

Sabrina has a method for learning quickly.
A method is a way of doing things.

1783   method

il metronomo

1784   metronome

il microfono

1785   microphone

il microscopio

1786   microscope

il forno a microonde

1787   microwave oven

mezzogiorno	**nel mezzo**	**il nano**	**mezzanotte**
1788 midday	1789 in the **middle**	1790 midget	1791 midnight

il miglio

Un miglio equivale a 1,6 chilometri.
Il limite di velocità è di 30 **miglia all'ora.**

*One mile equals 1.6 kilometers.
The speed limit is 30 miles per hour.*

1792   mile

il latte di mucca

1793   milk

Il mulino è sulla riva del fiume.

1794   mill

la mente, l'intelligenza

$E = MC^2$

1795   mind

La miniera è sotto terra.

1796   mine

Il minatore lavora nella miniera.

1797   miner

i minerali

1798   minerals

il pesciolino

1799   minnow

La menta è una pianta aromatica.

1800   mint

Sette **meno** cinque, uguale due.

$7 - 5 = 2$

1801   minus

Vi sono 60 **minuti** in un'ora.

1802   minute

uno strano **miracolo**

1803   miracle

il miraggio nel deserto

1804   mirage

lo specchio

1805   mirror

L'avaro tiene tutto per sè.

1806   miser

Sento la mancanza della mia famiglia.

1807   to miss

il missile

1808   missile

Michele si è perso a causa della **foschia**.

1809   mist

il vischio

1810   mistletoe

le manopole, i guanti

1811   mittens

mescolare

1812   to mix

il frullatore

1813   mixer

il fossato attorno al castello

1814   moat

L'uccello **si burla** del gatto.

1815   to mock

il tordo beffeggiatore

1816   mockingbird

il modello di aereo

1817   model airplane/aeroplane*

una sedia **moderna**

1818   modern chair

Ha il pannolino **umido**.

1819   moist

la talpa

1820   mole

il neo di bellezza

1821   mole

Un momento, per favore!

1822   One **moment** please.

lunedì

Lunedì è il primo giorno della settimana.

Monday is the first day of the week.

1823   Monday

il denaro

1824   money

la scimmia

1825   monkey

l'angelo di mare

1826   monkfish

Che orribile **mostro**!

1827   monster

Vi sono dodici **mesi** in un anno.

1828   month

un monumento al capo

1829   monument

E' di buon **umore**.

1830   He is in a good **mood**.

E' di cattivo **umore**.

1831   He is in a bad **mood**.

una falce di **luna**

1832   moon

un alce americano

1833   moose

il mattino

1834   morning

il mortaio con il pestello

1835   **mortar** and pestle

il mosaico

1836   mosaic

La zanzara punge.

1837   mosquito

Il muschio cresce all'ombra.

1838   moss

la mamma, la madre

1839   mother

il motore elettrico

1840   motor

la motocicletta

1841   motorcycle

lo stampo per i dolci

1842   mould*/mold

il monticello

1843   mound

montare in sella

1844   to mount

la montagna

1845   mountain

il topo

1846   mouse

i baffi

1847   moustache*/mustache

la bocca

1848   mouth

La lumaca **si muove** lentamente.

1849   to move

il movimento del pendolo

1850   movement

il cinema, la sala cinematografica

1851   movie/film*

falciare l'erba del prato

1852   to **mow** the lawn

E' **troppo** per me.

1853   too **much** for me

Perché è seduto nel **fango**?

1854   mud

il mulo

1855   mule

moltiplicare

1856   multiply

Maurizio ha **gli orecchioni**.

1857   mumps

Uccidere qualcuno è un crimine terribile.

1858   to murder

il muscolo

1859   muscle

il museo

1860   museum

Alcuni **funghi** sono velenosi.

1861   mushroom

A Sabrina piace **la musica**.

1862   music

La mamma di Sabrina è **una musicista**.

1863   musician

Le cozze vivono nel mare.

1864   mussel

Devi saltare.

1865   You **must** jump.

la mostarda, la salsa di senape

1866   mustard

Ha **la museruola** sul **muso**.

1867   muzzle

il chiodo

1868   nail

un'unghia

1869   finger**nail**

forbicine per le unghie

1870   **nail** clipper

Sono ambedue **nudi**.

1872   naked

Il mio nome è . . .

1873   My **name** is . . .

il tovagliolo, la salvietta

1874   napkin/serviette*

inchiodare

1871   to **nail**

troppo **stretto** per passarvi

1875   too **narrow** to pass

L'Islanda è **una nazione**.

1876   nation

naturale

Gli alimenti **naturali** fanno
bene alla salute.
La frutta contiene zucchero
naturale.

*It is healthy to eat
natural foods.
Fruit contains natural sugar.*

1877   natural

La natura è meravigliosa.

1878   nature

La ragazzina è **cattiva**.

1879   She is **naughty**.

navigare

1880   to **navigate**

sempre più **vicino**

1881   near

lindo, accurato

1882   neat

non piacevole, ma
necessario

1883   Not pleasant, but **necessary**.

il collo

1884   neck

la collana

1885   necklace

Le api fanno il miele con **il
nettare**.

1886   nectar

la pesca-noce

1887   nectarine

il bisogno, la necessità

Sabrina aiuta sempre gli amici nel **bisogno**.
Il cibo e l'abitazione sono **necessità** fondamentali.

Sabrina always helps her friends in need.
Food and shelter are basic needs.

1888   need

Ho bisogno di un bicchier d'acqua.

1889   I need water.

Sei capace di infilare l'ago?

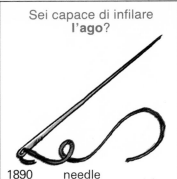

1890   needle

Trascura il suo cane.

1891   He neglects his dog.

Il cavallo nitrisce.

1892   to neigh

i vicini

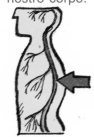

1893   neighbors/neighbours*

Né l'una, né l'altra mi va bene.

1894   neither one fits

---

un'insegna al neon

1895   neon sign

Mio nipote è figlio di mio fratello.

1896   My nephew is my brother's son.

Abbiamo molti nervi nel nostro corpo.

1897   nerve

Roberto è nervoso.

1898   nervous

---

due uova nel nido

1899   nest

Le ortiche pungono.

1900   nettle

Non giocare mai con il fuoco.

1901   Never play with fire!

un cappello nuovo

1902   new

---

le notizie

Mamma legge **le notizie**.
Ho buone **notizie** per te.
Hai **notizie** da casa?

Mom reads the news.
I have good news for you.
Any news from home?

1903   news

il giornale

1904   newspaper

Avanti il prossimo!

1905   Next !

Lo scoiattolo rosicchia una nocciuola.

1906   to nibble

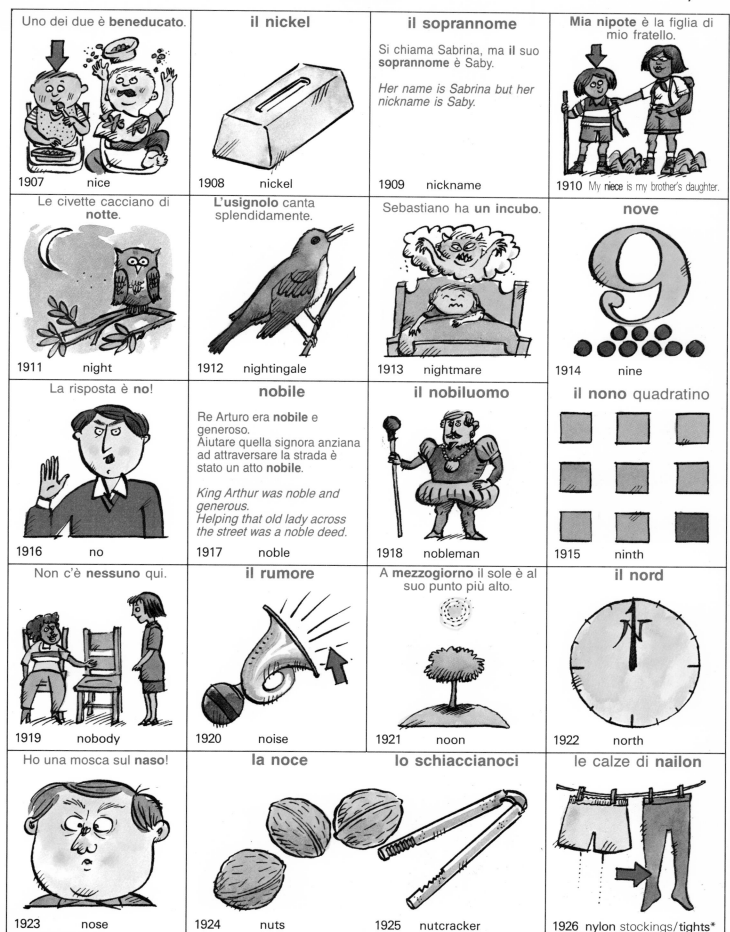

Uno dei due è **beneducato**.

1907　　nice

il nickel

1908　　nickel

il soprannome

Si chiama Sabrina, ma **il** suo **soprannome** è Saby.

Her name is Sabrina but her nickname is Saby.

1909　　nickname

Mia nipote è la figlia di mio fratello.

1910　My **niece** is my brother's daughter.

Le civette cacciano di **notte**.

1911　　night

L'usignolo canta splendidamente.

1912　　nightingale

Sebastiano ha **un incubo**.

1913　　nightmare

nove

1914　　nine

La risposta è **no**!

1916　　no

nobile

Re Arturo era **nobile** e generoso.
Aiutare quella signora anziana ad attraversare la strada è stato un atto **nobile**.

King Arthur was noble and generous.
Helping that old lady across the street was a noble deed.

1917　　noble

il nobiluomo

1918　　nobleman

il nono quadratino

1915　　ninth

Non c'è **nessuno** qui.

1919　　nobody

il rumore

1920　　noise

A **mezzogiorno** il sole è al suo punto più alto.

1921　　noon

il nord

1922　　north

Ho una mosca sul **naso**!

1923　　nose

la noce

1924　　nuts

lo schiaccianoci

1925　　nutcracker

le calze di **nailon**

1926　nylon stockings/**tights***

la quercia

1927   oak

A quello squalo piacciono **i remi!**

1928   oar

un'oasi nel deserto

1929   oasis

oblungo

1930   oblong

osservare

1931   to observe

Le navi attraversano **l'oceano**.

1932   ocean

Un ottagono ha otto lati.

1933   octagon

Ottobre è il decimo mese dell'anno.

1934   October

il polipo, la piovra

1935   octopus

il contachilometri

1936   odometer/milometer*

un odore insopportabile

1937   odor/odour*

Scendi dalla tavola!
La luce è spenta.
Togliti il cappotto.

Get off the table!
The light is off.
Take off your coat.

1938   off

Quest'uomo **offre** a Lino del denaro per la mucca.

1939   to offer

un ufficiale

1940   officer

sovente, spesso

D'autunno piove **sovente**.
L'autobus passa **spesso**?
Abbastanza **sovente**.

It often rains in the fall.
Does the bus run often?
Often enough.

1941   often

l'olio, il petrolio

1942   oil

l'unguento, la pomata

1943   ointment

un uomo molto **vecchio**

1944   old

Le olive maturano sugli alberi.

1945   olive

Il cuoco fa **una frittata**.

1946   omelette

Il vaso di fiori è **sul** tavolo.

1947   on the table

una volta

C'era **una volta** una bambina chiamata Sabrina...
Mario è andato al campeggio solo **una volta**.

Once upon a time, there was a little girl called Sabrina...
Mario has been to camp only once.

1948   once

il numero uno

1949   one

la cipolla

1950   onion

mio **unico** amore

1951   my **only** love

Non lasciare la porta **aperta**.

1952   open

aprire

1953   to open

un'operazione

1954   operation

un opossum

1955   opossum

opposto, dirimpetto

Il bene è **l'opposto** del male.
Venivano dalla direzione **opposta**.
I Rossi abitano **dirimpetto** a noi.

Good is the opposite of bad.
They came from the opposite direction.
The Rossis live opposite us.

1956   opposite

o, oppure

Vuoi una mela **o** una pera?
Puoi fare il compito **oppure** lavare i piatti.

Do you prefer an apple or a pear?
You can do your homework or wash the dishes.

1957   or

Bisogna pelare **l'arancia**.

1958   orange

il color **arancione**

1959   orange

Il frutteto è pieno di alberi da frutta.

1960   orchard

un'orchestra

1961   orchestra

un'orchidea

1962   orchid

Il signor Edoardo **ordina** la cena.

1963   to order

l'origano

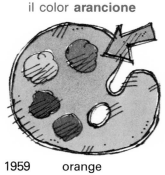

1964   oregano

Alberto suona **l'organo**.

1965   organ

il rigogolo, l'oriolo

1966   oriole

Un orfano non ha genitori.

1967   orphan

Lo struzzo è un uccello che non vola.

1968   ostrich

La lontra è abilissima nel prendere i pesci.

1969   otter

Dodici **once** fanno una libbra.

1970   ounce

fuori, all'aria aperta

1971   outdoors

Ti piace **il** mio **vestito**?

1972   outfit

ovale

1973   oval

C'è una focaccia nel **forno**.

1974   oven

Uomo **in mare**!

1975   Man **overboard**!

il soprabito

1976   overcoat

Il secchio **trabocca**.

1977   to **overflow**

la soprascarpa, la caloscia

1978   overshoe

capovolgere, rovesciarsi

1979   to **overturn**

essere in debito, dovere

E' meglio non **essere in debito** con nessuno.
Dobbiamo molto ai nostri genitori.

It is best not to owe any money.
We owe a great deal to our parents.

1980   to **owe**

il gufo

1981   owl

avere, possedere

La famiglia Bianchi **ha** una villetta al mare.
Possediamo la casa in cui abitiamo.

The Bianchi family owns a house at the seaside.
We own the house we live in.

1982   to **own**

il bue

1983   ox

Il palombaro ha bisogno di **ossigeno**.

1984   oxygen

un'ostrica

1985   oyster

P

Sabrina **fa le valigie**.

1986   to pack

il pacco

1987   package

il blocchetto di fogli, il bloc-notes

1988   pad

Isabella tiene **la pagaia** ben stretta.

1990   paddle

Non sa **remare** molto bene.

1991   to paddle

il lucchetto

1992   padlock

la rampa di lancio

1989   pad

Gira **la pagina**!

1993   page

Il secchio è pieno e pesante.

1994   pail

la vernice, la tinta

1996   paint

Vernice fresca.

1997   wet paint

Tommaso si è fatto male e sente un certo **dolore**.

1995   pain

il decoratore, l'imbianchino

2000   painter

Nicola **vernicia** lo steccato.

1998   to paint

il pennello

1999   paintbrush

il quadro

2001   painting

un paio di scarpe

2002   a pair of shoes

il palazzo

2003   palace

Questo fiore è d'un colore **pallido**.

2004   pale

la tavolozza del pittore	**il palmo** della mano	**la teglia**	**la frittella**
2005 palette	2006 palm	2007 pan	2008 pancake
il panda	**il pannello** dei comandi	Fabrizio suona **la siringa**.	**la viola del pensiero**
2009 panda	2010 panel	2011 panpipe	2012 pansy
Il cane **ansima**.	**la pantera**	**i pantaloni**	**La papaia** è un frutto commestibile.
2013 to pant	2014 panther	2015 pants/trousers*	2016 papaya
la carta	**Il paracadute** frena la caduta.	**la parata**	linee **parallele**
2017 paper	2018 parachute	2019 parade	2020 parallel lines
Il topolino è **paralizzato** dalla paura.	Sabrina ha ricevuto **un pacco**.	**Un genitore** è un papà o una mamma.	Alla nonna piacciono molto **i parchi**.
2021 paralyzed/paralysed*	2022 parcel	2023 parent	2024 park

parcheggiare	**la giacca a vento**	**il parlamento**	**Il pappagallo** ripete tutto quel che dico.
2025 to park	2026 parka	2027 parliament	2028 parrot
il prezzemolo	**La pastinaca** produce una radice commestibile.	Ci sono dei **granelli** di polvere nell'aria.	**il cavaliere, la dama**
2029 parsley	2030 parsnip	2031 particle	2032 partner
la festa, il ricevimento	Maria **passa** la palla...	... e Felice **sviene** dal colpo.	**il corridoio**
2033 party	2034 to pass	2035 to pass out	2036 passage
Sabrina ama **le feste**.	Per viaggiare all'estero occorre **il passaporto**.	**passato**	**la pasta, la pastasciutta**
		Nel **passato** non v'erano né automobili né aeroplani. Ieri è il **passato**; domani è il futuro. *In the past, there were no planes or cars. Yesterday is the past; tomorrow is the future.*	
2037 passenger	2038 passport	2039 past	2040 pasta
Il signor Bianchi **incolla** la carta da parati.	Il ricamo è **il passatempo** preferito di Maria.	**la pasticceria, le paste**	Le pecore brucano l'erba nel **pascolo**.
2041 to paste	2042 pastime	2043 pastry	2044 pasture

una toppa ben visibile

2045   patch

il sentiero, la via

2046   path

La bambina è **paziente**.

2047   She is patient.

Il paziente sembra un po' nervoso.

2048   patient

il modello in carta

2049   pattern

fare una pausa, fermarsi

Dopo aver letto due pagine, Sabrina **fece una pausa**. Devo **fermarmi** un momento per riprendere fiato.

After reading two pages, Sabrina paused. I have to pause for breath.

2050   to pause

camminare sul **selciato**

2051   pavement/road*

Quante **zampe** ha il gatto?

2052   paw

I genitori hanno molti conti da **pagare**.

2053   to pay

il telefono **a pagamento**

2054 pay phone/phone box*

Pace in terra!

2055   peace

La pesca ha la pelle vellutata.

2056   peach

Il pavone fa la ruota.

2057   peacock

il picco, la vetta

2058   peak

lo **scampanio**, il suono delle campane

2059   peal of a bell

l'arachide, la nocciolina americana

2060   peanut

la pera

2061   pear

La perla è nascosta nell'ostrica.

2062   pearl

I piselli sono racchiusi nel baccello.

2063   peas

la torba per il giardinaggio

2064   peat moss

i ciottoli, i sassolini	**la noce americana**
2065　pebbles	2066　pecan

beccare	**il pedale** della bicicletta
2067　to peck	2068　pedal

Il pedone cammina sul marciapiede.	**il passaggio pedonale**
2070　pedestrian	2071　pedestrian crossing

pelare, sbucciare	**pedalare**
2072　to peel	2069　to pedal

Il pellicano ha il becco molto lungo.	**la penna** a sfera
2073　pelican	2074　pen

la matita	**Il pendolo** oscilla da destra a sinistra.
2075　pencil	2076　pendulum

Il pinguino ha il piumaggio bianco e nero.	**il temperino**
2077　penguin	2078　penknife

Il pentagono ha cinque lati.	**la gente**
2079　pentagon	2080　people

I grani di **pepe** sono accanto al macinino.	**la menta peperita**
2081　pepper	2082　peppermint

il pesce persico	L'uccello ha trovato **un posatoio**.
2083　perch	2084　perch

un'ottima **prestazione**

2085   performance

il profumo

2086   perfume

Si mette **un punto fermo** alla fine di ogni periodo.

glurg↓

2087   period/full stop*

La pervinca ha fiori violacei.

2088   periwinkle

la persona

2089   person

un insetto nocivo

2090   pest

Gaetano **importuna** suo padre.

2091   to pester

il suo **animale favorito**

2092   pet

Quanti **petali** ha questo fiore?

2094   petal

la petunia

2095   petunia

La farmacista vende medicinali.

2096   pharmacist/chemist*

coccolare, accarezzare

2093   to pet

la farmacia

2097   pharmacy/chemist's*

il fagiano

2098   pheasant

il telefono

2099   phone

la fotografia, **la foto**

2100   photograph

il pianoforte della mamma di Sabrina

2101   piano

Scegli una carta!

2102   to pick

prendere su, sollevare

2103   to pick up

il piccone

2104   pickaxe

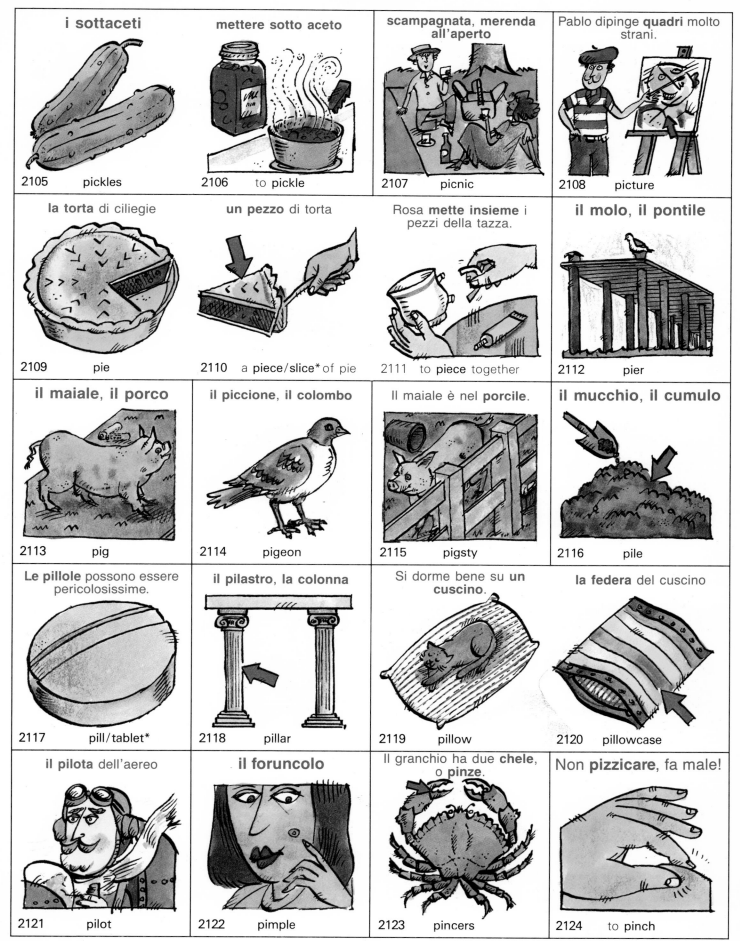

i sottaceti
2105   pickles

mettere sotto aceto
2106   to pickle

scampagnata, merenda all'aperto
2107   picnic

Pablo dipinge **quadri** molto strani.
2108   picture

la torta di ciliegie
2109   pie

un pezzo di torta
2110   a piece/slice* of pie

Rosa **mette insieme** i pezzi della tazza.
2111   to piece together

il molo, il pontile
2112   pier

il maiale, il porco
2113   pig

il piccione, il colombo
2114   pigeon

Il maiale è nel **porcile**.
2115   pigsty

il mucchio, il cumulo
2116   pile

Le pillole possono essere pericolosissime.
2117   pill/tablet*

il pilastro, la colonna
2118   pillar

Si dorme bene su **un cuscino**.
2119   pillow

la federa del cuscino
2120   pillowcase

il pilota dell'aereo
2121   pilot

il foruncolo
2122   pimple

Il granchio ha due **chele**, o **pinze**.
2123   pincers

Non **pizzicare**, fa male!
2124   to pinch

il pino

2125   pine

un ananas

2126   pineapple

il color **rosa**

2127   pink

Il nonno fuma **la pipa**.

2128   pipe

un vecchio **pirata**

2129   pirate

il pistacchio

2130   pistachio

una pistola molto antica

2131   pistol

Giorgio **lancia la palla**.

2132   to pitch

compassionare

Sabrina **compassiona** Luca, che ha perso il gatto.

Sabrina pities Luca, who has lost his cat.

2136   to pity

posto

Non c'è nessun **posto** come casa propria.
Giovanni rimette il martello a **posto**.

*There is no place like home.
Giovanni puts the hammer in its place.*

2137   place

la pianuzza, la passera di mare

2138   plaice

lancio, tono

Bravo Giorgio, **un** bel **lancio**!
Questo piano è fuori **tono**.

*Bravo Giorgio, that was a good pitch!
This piano is off pitch.*

2133   pitch

Lei ha una camicetta **non lavorata**.

2139   plain shirt

la pianura

2140   plain

L'architetto **progetta** una casa.

2141   to plan

il forcone

2134   pitchfork

la pialla del falegname

2142   plane

I pianeti girano attorno al sole.

2143   planets

la tavola, **l'asse**

2144   plank

la pece

2135   pitch tar

la pianta   **piantare**

2145   plants   2146   to plant

intonaco, stucco   L'operaia **intonaca** il muro.

2147   plaster   2148   to plaster

la plastica

2149   plastic

la plastilina

2150   plasticine

Questo è **il piatto** di Sabrina.

2151   plate

un altipiano

2152   plateau

la banchina della stazione

2153   platform

I bambini **giocano** nella sabbia.

2154   to play

un campo-giuochi

2155   playground

le carte da giuoco

2156   playing cards

supplicare il carnefice

2157   to plead

una giornata **piacevole**

2158   a pleasant day

Un bicchier di latte, **per favore**.

2159 A glass of milk, **please**.

le pieghe del gonnellino

2160   pleat

le pinze

2161   pliers

Il contadino ara la terra con **un aratro**.

2162   plow/plough*

spennare un volatile

2163   to pluck

inserire **la spina** nella presa

2164   plug

il tappo del lavandino

2165   plug

la susina, la prugna

2166   plum

l'idraulico

2167   plumber

Grassoccio, paffuto

2168   plump

il plurale

'Libri' è **il plurale** di 'libro'. 'Uno' è singolare, 'molti' è **plurale**.

'Books' is the plural of 'book'. 'One' is singular, 'many' is plural.

2169   plural

Uno **più** uno uguale...

2170   plus

il legno compensato

2171   plywood

Il cuoco **fa le uova in camicia.**

2172   to poach

la tasca

2173   pocket

il baccello dei piselli

2174   pea pod

la poesia, il poema

Una **poesia** è fatta di versi. Dante scrisse **poemi** diversi.

A poem consists of verses. Dante wrote various poems.

2175   poem

indicare, additare

2177   to point

la poinsezia, la stella di Natale

2176   poinsettia

il veleno

2180   poison

velenoso

Certi tipi di funghi sono **velenosi**. La maggior parte dei serpenti non sono **velenosi**.

Some mushrooms are poisonous. Most snakes are not poisonous.

2181   poisonous

La punta della freccia è di metallo.

2178   point

colpire, spingere colla mano

2182   to poke

un orso polare

2183   polar bear

il palo del telefono

2184   pole

Questo legno è **appuntito**.

2179   pointed

il poliziotto, l'agente di polizia

2185　policeman

la donna poliziotto

2186　policewoman

lucidare, levigare

2187　to polish

ben educato, cortese

Gridare non è da persona **ben educata**.
L'insegnante si aspetta una risposta **cortese**.

It is not polite to shout.
The teacher expects a polite answer.

2188　polite

il polline dei fiori

2189　pollen

La melagrana è un frutto.

2190　pomegranate

uno stagno in mezzo al bosco

2191　pond

il pony di Donatella

2192　pony

Nuotano nella **piscina**.

2193　pool

mettere in comune

2194　to pool

povero, scadente

La sua famiglia non è **povera**, ma non è neppure ricca.
Sabrina ha riportato voti **scadenti**, perché non ha studiato molto.

Her family is not poor, but it is not rich either.
Sabrina had poor results because she did not work hard.

2195　poor

far saltare il tappo

2196　to pop

il pioppo

2197　poplar

il papavero

2198　poppy

ben voluto, in voga

L'insegnante di Sabrina è **ben voluto** dai suoi alunni.
Questa canzone era **in voga** l'estate scorsa.

Sabrina's teacher is popular with his pupils.
This song was popular last summer.

2199　popular

la veranda

2200　porch

I pori sono piccoli fori nella pelle.

2201　Pores are little holes in the skin.

la pappa d'avena

2202　porridge

il porto

2203　port

portatile

Sabrina vorrebbe una radio **portatile**, ma non ha risparmiato abbastanza per comprarla.

Sabrina wants a portable radio but she has not saved up enough money.

2204　portable

**il facchino,
il portabagagli**

2205   porter

il ritratto di zia Carolina

2206   portrait

il palo, il pilastro

2207   post

Franco **imbuca** una lettera.

2208   to post

la cartolina postale

2210   postcard

il manifesto, il cartellone

2211   poster

la pentola

2212   pot

l'ufficio postale

2209   post office

la patata

2213   potato

le ceramiche, le terraglie

2214   pottery

la borsa, il sacchetto

2215   pouch

**balzare, piombare
addosso**

2216   to pounce

la libbra, il canile

Quattro banane pesano circa
una libbra.
I cani randagi vengono portati
al **canile** municipale.

*Four bananas weigh about a
pound.
Stray dogs are taken to the dog
pound.*

2217   pound

battere, pestare

2218   to pound

versare

2219   to pour

fare il broncio

2220   to pout

la polvere

2221   powder

**esercitarsi, mettere in
pratica**

2222   to practice/practise*

Le praterie canadesi
producono molto grano.

2223   prairie

elogiare, esaltare

2224   to praise

Il cavallo **si impenna**.	**pregare**	Io **preferisco** questo.	La donna è **incinta**.
2225 to prance	2226 to pray	2227 to prefer	2228 She is **pregnant**.
Io sono **presente**.	**il regalo** per il compleanno	**presentare, consegnare** un premio	**la composta** di frutta
2229 I am **present**.	2230 birthday **present**	2231 to present	2232 preserved fruit
premere il bottone	**una bambina** graziosa	La civetta ha **la preda** tra gli artigli.	**Il prezzo** è segnato sul cartellino.
2233 to press	2234 pretty	2235 prey	2236 price
pungere	un animale **munito di aculei**	una scuola **elementare**	**la primula**
2237 to prick	2238 prickly animal	2239 primary school	2240 primrose
il principe	**la principessa**	**la preside** della scuola	**il principio, la teoria**

il principio, la teoria

Il **principio** fondamentale è quello di lavorare assiduamente.
In teoria, sono d'accordo con te.

The first principle is to work hard.
In principle, I agree with you.

2241 prince	2242 princess	2243 school principal/Head teacher*	2244 principle

stampare

2245 to print

Il **prisma** separa i colori della luce.

2246 prism

Il ladro è in **prigione** per i crimini che ha commesso.

2247 prison

il detenuto

2248 prisoner

privato

Sabrina ed io siamo impegnate in una conversazione **privata**. Questa è una proprietà **privata**.

Sabrina and I are having a private conversation.
This is private property.

2249 private

il premio

2250 prize

il problema

2251 problem

i **prodotti** agricoli

2252 produce

Sono pochi **i programmi** televisivi interessanti.

2254 program/programme*

vietato ai cani

2255 prohibited

il progetto

Debora sta lavorando a **un progetto** difficile.
Sabrina non ha avuto buoni risultati con il suo **progetto**.

Debora is working on a difficult project.
Sabrina did not do well on her project.

2256 project

Questa fabbrica **produce** automobili.

2253 This factory **produces** cars.

Lo prometto!

2257 I promise.

il dente del forcone

2258 prong

Pronuncia le parole chiaramente.

2259 to pronounce

la prova del delitto

2260 proof of guilt

puntellare, sostenere

2261 to prop

l'elica dell'aeroplano

2262 propeller

vestito **con proprietà**

2263 properly dressed

proprietà

Sabrina dice "E' mio" quando vuol dire "Questo è di mia **proprietà**".
La sua famiglia possiede **una proprietà** in campagna.

Sabrina says "This is mine" when she means "This is my property".
Her family owns property in the country.

2264 property

protestare	La gatta è **fiera** dei suoi piccoli.	Lo posso **provare**.	**il proverbio**
			Come dice **il proverbio**, can che abbaia non morde. *As the proverb goes, his bark is worse than his bite.*
2265 to **protest**	2266 I am a **proud** cat.	2267 to **prove**	2268 **proverb**
provvedere, mettere a disposizione	**La prugna** è il frutto del susino.	**potare**	il telefono **pubblico**
2269 to **provide** chairs	2270 **prune**	2271 to **prune**	2272 **public** telephone/phone box*
il budino	**la pozzanghera**	**sbuffare, tirar boccate di fumo**	**la pulcinella di mare**
2273 **pudding**/afters*	2274 **puddle**	2275 to **puff**	2276 **puffin**
tirare	**la puleggia, la carrucola**	**il maglione, il pullover**	Il medico controlla **il polso** a Sabrina.
2277 to **pull**	2278 **pulley**	2279 **pullover**/sweater*	2280 **pulse**
la pompa	**pompare, gonfiare**	**la zucca**	**colpire con un pugno**
2281 **pump**	2282 to **pump**	2283 **pumpkin**	2284 to **punch**

2285 — Lei è **puntuale.** — You are **punctual.**

2286 — Piero sarà punito per **aver forato** la gomma. — to **puncture**

2287 — La maestra **punisce** la scolara cattiva. — to **punish**

2288 — **la punizione** — **punishment**

2289 — **la marionetta** — **puppet**

2290 — **il cucciolo** — **puppy**

2291 — l'acqua **pura** — **pure** water

2292 — **violetto** — **purple**

2293 — I gatti **fanno le fusa** quando sono contenti. — to **purr**

2294 — **la borsetta** — **purse/handbag***

2295 — Fido **insegue** Tigre. — to **pursue**

2296 — **spingere** — to **push**

2297 — **mettere, porre** — to **put**

2298 — **Mette via** gli indumenti nel cassetto. — to **put away**

2299 — **Rinvia** la lettura a più tardi. — to **put off**

2300 — **Il mastice** sigilla i vetri della finestra. — **putty**

2301 — **il rompicapo** — **puzzle**

2302 — **il pigiama** — **pyjamas*/pajamas**

2303 — **la piramide** — **pyramid**

2304 — **Il pitone** soffoca la preda tra le sue spire. — **python**

la quaglia

2305   quail

un orologio di buona **qualità**

2306   quality watch

la quantità

2307   quantity

bisticciare, altercare

2308   to quarrel

E' **una cava** di pietre o **una cava** di sabbia?

2309   quarry

un quarto

$\frac{1}{4}$

2310   quarter

La barca è accostata alla **banchina.**

2311   quay

la regina

2312   queen

fare **una domanda**

2313   to ask a question

rapido come il lampo

2314   quick

Sta affondando nelle **sabbie mobili.**

2315   quicksand

Lei è **quieta.**

2316   She is quiet.

In altri tempi si scriveva con **una penna d'oca.**

2317   quill

Il porcospino ha **aculei** per difendersi.

2318   porcupine quill

la coperta imbottita

2319   quilt/eiderdown*

la mela cotogna

2320   quince

una faretra piena di frecce

2321   quiver

tremare, rabbrividire

2322   to quiver

il questionario, l'esame

Ieri abbiamo risposto a **un questionario** di storia.
Oggi avremo **un esame** di geografia.

Yesterday, we had a history quiz.
Today we are going to have a geography quiz.

2323   quiz

R

il coniglio
2324   rabbit

il procione
2325   raccoon

La lepre e la tartaruga **fanno la corsa**.
2326   to race

l'attaccapanni
2327   rack/hat-stand*

il frastuono, il fracasso
2328   racket

Il radiatore riscalda la stanza.
2329   radiator

la radio
2330   radio

il ravanello
2331   radish

il raggio del cerchio
2332   radius

La zattera galleggia sull'acqua.
2333   raft

Un'incursione in corso.
2334   a raid in progress

Tienti bene al **corrimano**.
2335   handrail/banister*

i binari della ferrovia
2336   railroad track/railway track*

piove a dirotto
2337   to rain

Dopo la pioggia viene **l'arcobaleno**.
2338   rainbow

un impermeabile
2339   raincoat

alzare, sollevare

Tutti quelli che vogliono del cioccolato **alzino** la mano.
Ha sollevato una questione molto interessante.

Everyone who wants chocolate, raise your hand!
She has raised an interesting question.

2340   to raise

l'uva passa
2341   raisin

il rastrello
2342   rake

bussare alla porta	**rapido**	**raro**	un'**eruzione** della pelle
2343 to rap/knock*	2344 rapid	2345 rare	2346 rash
I lamponi crescono su piccoli arbusti.	**il ratto**	**il sonaglio** del bambino	**il serpente a sonagli**
2347 raspberry	2348 rat	2349 rattle	2350 rattlesnake
Il corvo ha il piumaggio nero.	ragazza **famelica**	**il burrone**	un uovo **crudo**
2351 raven	2352 ravenous	2353 ravine	2354 a raw egg
un raggio di sole	La lama del **rasoio** è molto affilata.	**raggiungere**	**leggere**
2355 ray of sunlight	2356 razor	2357 to reach	2358 to read
Ai vostri posti...**pronti**...via!	Si tratta di un diamante **vero**?	**comprendere, rendersi conto**	Sei **davvero** tornato?
2359 ready	2360 real	2361 to realize/realise*	2362 Are you **really** here?

il deretano, il di dietro

2363   rear

lo specchietto retrovisore

2364   rearview mirror

ragionare, argomentare

2365   to reason

ragionevole

E' un prezzo **ragionevole**.
Sabrina, sii **ragionevole**, per favore!

*That is a reasonable price.
Sabrina, be reasonable, please!*

2366   reasonable

---

ribellarsi, rivoltarsi

La gente **si ribella** contro le ingiustizie.
Spartaco **si rivoltò** contro Roma.

*People rebel against injustice.
Spartacus rebelled against Rome.*

2367   to rebel

Non **mi ricordo**.

2368   I do not **recall**.

ricevere un regalo

2369   to receive

appena schiuso

2370   recently hatched

---

la ricetta

2371   recipe

Sta recitando una poesia.

2372   to recite

il disco, il documento

2373   record

il giradischi

2374   record player

---

guarire, recuperare

Sabrina ha il morbillo, ma **guarirà** presto.
Ho recuperato tutti i libri che erano rimasti fuori.

*Sabrina has measles but she will recover soon.
I recovered all the books that were left outside.*

2375   to recover

il rettangolo

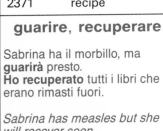

2376   rectangle

rosso

2377   red

la canna

2378   reed

---

il banco di corallo, la scogliera corallina

2379   reef

Quanto **puzza**!

2380   to reek

La lenza è avvolta sul **mulinello**.

2381   reel

un arbitro

2382   referee

il riflesso, l'immagine riflessa	Non lasciare **il frigorifero** aperto!	**rifiutare**	**la regione**
2383 reflection	2384 refrigerator	2385 to refuse	2386 region
iscriversi	**rimpiangere**	Gli attori **fanno le prove**.	**la renna**
2387 to register	2388 to regret	2389 Actors rehearse a play.	2390 reindeer
le **redini** del cavallo	**i parenti**	riposare, rilassarsi	**rilasciare, liberare**
2391 reins	2392 relatives	2393 to relax	2394 to release
Ricordati di lavarti i denti!	un'isoletta **remota**	Filippo **si toglie** il cappello.	**affittare** **Affittiamo** un appartamento. Se non hai la macchina, ne puoi **affittare** una. *We rent an apartment. If you do not have a car, you can rent one.*
2395 Remember to brush your teeth.	2396 remote island	2397 to remove	2398 to rent
Annamaria si **ripara** la bicicletta.	Il pappagallo **ripete** tutto.	Giovanna **sostituisce** la lampadina.	Lui domanda, lei **risponde**.
2399 to repair	2400 to repeat	2401 to replace	2402 to reply

il rettile

2403 reptile

salvare, soccorrere

2404 to rescue

il serbatoio

2405 reservoir

responsabile

Sabrina, sei **responsabile** di tuo fratello.
Papà vide il latte versato e chiese: ''Chi è **il responsabile**?''

Sabrina, you are responsible for your little brother.
Dad saw the spilled milk and asked: "Who is responsible for this?"

2406 responsible

Paolo **si riposa** nella sua poltrona.

2407 to rest

il ristorante

2408 restaurant

restituire, ritornare

Sabrina **restituisce** sempre i libri della biblioteca.
Giovanni è in viaggio, ma **ritornerà** presto.

Sabrina always returns her library books.
Giavonni is travelling but he will return soon.

2409 to return

Battista **fa marcia indietro**.

2410 reverse

---

il rinoceronte

2411 rhinoceros

il rabarbaro

2412 rhubarb

la rima

Cuore fa **rima** con amore.
Cerca una parola che fa **rima** con...

'Cuore' rhymes with 'amore'.
Find a word that rhymes with...

2413 rhyme

la costola

2414 rib

Sei capace di fare un fiocco con **un nastro**?

2415 ribbon

il riso

2416 rice

ricco

I ricchi devono aiutare i poveri.
Le arance sono **ricche** di vitamine.

The rich must help the poor.
Oranges are rich in vitamins.

2417 rich

Non sanno risolvere questo **enigma**.

2418 riddle

---

andare a cavallo

2419 to **ride** a horse

la cresta, la catena di monti

2420 ridge

la mano **destra**

2421 my **right** hand

destra, giusto

All'angolo, gira a **destra**.
Rubare non è **giusto**.

Turn right at the corner.
It is not right to steal.

2422 right

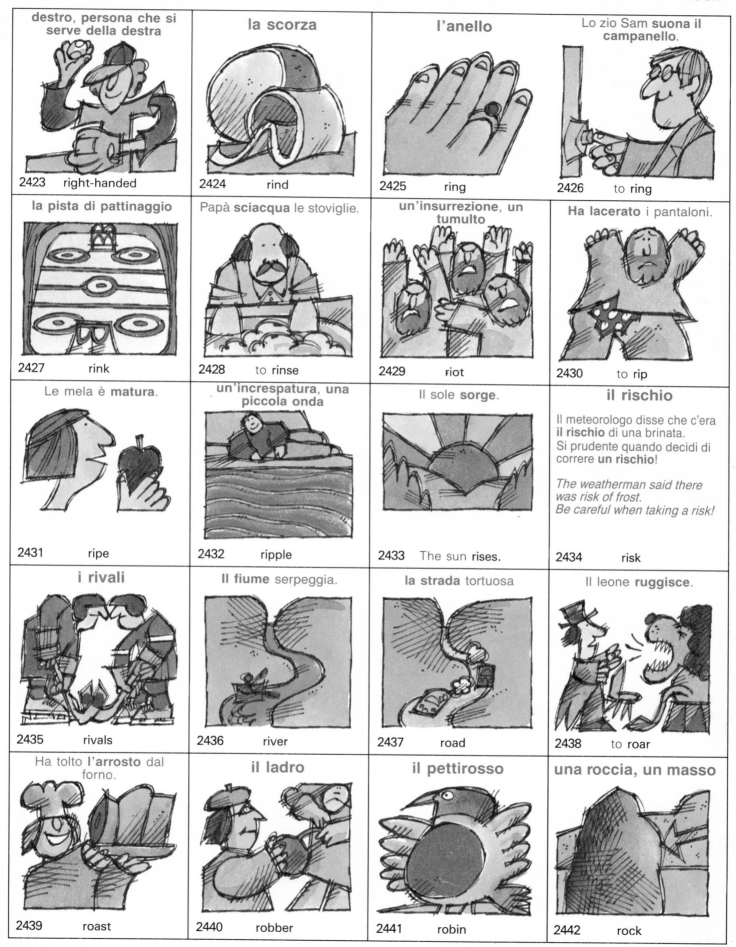

destro, persona che si serve della destra	la scorza	l'anello	Lo zio Sam **suona il campanello**.
2423 right-handed	2424 rind	2425 ring	2426 to ring
la pista di pattinaggio	Papà **sciacqua** le stoviglie.	un'insurrezione, un tumulto	**Ha lacerato** i pantaloni.
2427 rink	2428 to rinse	2429 riot	2430 to rip
Le mela è **matura**.	un'increspatura, una piccola onda	Il sole **sorge**.	il rischio
			Il meteorologo disse che c'era **il rischio** di una brinata. Si prudente quando decidi di correre **un rischio**! *The weatherman said there was risk of frost. Be careful when taking a risk!*
2431 ripe	2432 ripple	2433 The sun rises.	2434 risk
i rivali	Il fiume serpeggia.	la strada tortuosa	Il leone ruggisce.
2435 rivals	2436 river	2437 road	2438 to roar
Ha tolto l'arrosto dal forno.	il ladro	il pettirosso	una roccia, un masso
2439 roast	2440 robber	2441 robin	2442 rock

dondolare	**il razzo**	**la sedia a dondolo**	**la canna** da pesca
2443 to rock	2444 rocket	2445 rocking chair	2446 rod
il rotolo di carta	**rotolare**	**un pattino a rotelle**	**il mattarello**
2447 roll	2448 to roll	2449 roller skate	2450 rolling pin
Il **tetto** è fatto di tegole.	**la stanza**, **la camera**	Il gallo **si appollaia** per la notte.	**la radice**
2451 roof	2452 room	2453 to roost	2454 root
la corda	**La rosa** ha delle spine.	**il rosmarino**	Simona ha le guance **rosee**.
2455 rope	2456 rose	2457 rosemary	2458 rosy
La mela è **marcia**.	**ruvido**	Il bottone è **rotondo**.	**una fila** di quattro bottoni
2459 rotten apple	2460 rough	2461 round	2462 4 buttons in a row

Rema meglio di Luca.

2463   to row

regale

2464   royal

Il pneumatico e la palla sono di **gomma**.

2465   rubber

i rifiuti, le immondizie

2466   rubbish

Il rubino è una pietra rossa.

2467   ruby

il timone

2468   rudder

E' **maleducato**.

2469   He is **rude**.

un terreno **accidentato**

2470   **rugged** terrain

le rovine di un antico castello

2471   ruin

la regola, il dominio

Mamma e papà stabiliscono **le regole** di condotta in casa. Certi paesi sono sotto **il dominio** di un re.

Mom and Dad make the rules in this house.
Some countries are under the rule of a king.

2472   rule

il sovrano

2473   ruler

Sente **un brontolio** lontano.

2474   I hear a **rumble**.

correre

2475   to run

scappare, scampare

2476   to run away

investire

2477   to run over

esaurire le proprie energie

2478   to run out of energy

precipitarsi

2479   to rush

Il robot è coperto di **ruggine**.

2480   rust

un solco nella strada

2481   rut

La segale è una pianta simile al grano.

2482   rye

S

il sacco di farina

2483   sack

La verità è un principio **sacro**.

2484   Truth is a **sacred** principle.

triste

2485   sad

la sella

2486   saddle

Che cosa c'è nella **cassaforte**?

2487   safe

Il vento gonfia **la vela**.

2488   sail

il sailboard

2489   sailboard

La barca a vela scivola sul lago.

2490   sailboat/sailing boat*

il marinaio

2491   sailor

l'insalata

2492   salad

la svendita

2493   sale

il salmone

2494   salmon

il sale e il pepe

2495   salt

salutare, fare il saluto

2496   to salute

stesso, **identico**

2497   same

la sabbia

2498   sand

il sandalo

2499   sandal

Sabrina si è preparata **un panino**.

2500   sandwich

la linfa dell'albero

2501   sap

la sardina	il satellite	un vestito di **raso**	**sabato**
2502 sardine	2503 satellite	2504 satin dress	Il **sabato** è il sesto giorno della settimana. Al **sabato** Sabrina non va a scuola. *Saturday is the sixth day of the week. Sabrina does not go to school on Saturday.* 2505 Saturday

la salsa	la salsiccia	Io so **risparmiare** il denaro.	**La sega** ha i denti.
2506 sauce/gravy*	2507 sausage	2508 I save my money.	2509 saw

la segatura	**Io dico** quel che penso.	l'impalcatura	segare
2511 sawdust	2512 I say what I think.	2513 scaffolding	2510 to saw

scottare, ustionare	**La bilancia** ha due piatti.	**un pettine . . .** . . .molto gustoso	**il cuoio capelluto**
2514 to scald	2515 scale	2516 scallop	2517 scalp

Quest'uomo ha **una** grande **cicatrice**.	Prova un piacere malvagio a **spaventare** la gente.	**Lo spaventapasseri** serve a tener lontani gli uccelli.	**una sciarpa** molto morbida
2518 scar	2519 to scare	2520 scarecrow	2521 scarf

scarlatto

2522   scarlet

la scena del delitto

2523   scene of a crime

il paesaggio

2524   scenery

l'erudizione, la borsa di studio

2525   scholarship

la scuola del villaggio

2526   school

la goletta

2527   schooner

le forbici

2528   scissors

raccogliere, prendere con la paletta

2529   to scoop

la motoretta

2530   scooter

La carta è **bruciacchiata** dalla fiamma.

2531   scorched paper

segnare una rete

2532   to score

un esploratore

2533   scout

i pezzi di carta

2534   scraps of paper

una **scorticatura**, una **lacerazione**

2535   scrape

il raschietto

2536   scraper

il graffio, la graffiatura

2537   scratch

la zanzariera

2538   screen

la vite

2539   screw

il cacciavite

2540   screwdriver

lavare, fregare

2541   to scrub

Lo scultore lavora il marmo.
2542   sculptor

il cavalluccio marino
2543   seahorse

il **Mare** Adriatico
2544   Adriatic sea

il gabbiano
2545   seagull

la foca
2546   seal

la cucitura
2547   seam

Che cosa **cerca** nell'erba?
2548   to search

il riflettore
2549   searchlight

le stagioni
Le quattro **stagioni** dell'anno sono la primavera, l'estate, l'autunno e l'inverno.

The four seasons are: spring, summer, autumn and winter.
2550   seasons

il sedile
2551   seat

Sabrina ha allacciato **la cintura di sicurezza**.
2552   seatbelt

l'alga marina
2553   seaweed

il secondo
2554   second

Ho **un segreto**.
2555   I have a secret.

vedere
2556   to see

l'altalena
2557   see-saw

il seme
2558   seed

Sembra morto.
2559   It seems to be dead.

afferrare
2560   to seize

Sei **un egoista**.
2561   You are selfish.

Rebecca **vende** frutta.

2562 to **sell**

---

il semicerchio

2563 semicircle

---

mandare, spedire

2564 to **send**

---

una pelle delicata

2565 **sensitive** skin

---

la frase, la sentenza

Sei capace di fare **una frase** completa?
Il giudice ha pronunciato **la sentenza**: due anni di carcere.

Can you make a full sentence? The judge has issued the sentence: two years in jail.

2566 sentence

---

la sentinella

2567 sentry

In **settembre** maturano molte frutta.

2568 September

---

servire un pasto

2569 to **serve**

---

sette

2570 seven

---

la settima foca

2571 seventh

---

parecchi, vari

2572 several

Ella **cuce** con filo e ago.

2573 to **sew**

---

la macchina da cucire

2574 sewing machine

---

consunto, sciupato

2575 shabby

---

la baracca

2576 shack

---

un'ombra

2577 shadow

---

un cane **dal pelo lungo**

2578 shaggy

---

scuotere, agitare

2579 to **shake**

---

l'acqua **poco profonda**

2580 **shallow** water

Mamma si lava i capelli con **lo shampoo**.

2581 shampoo

Possiamo **spartirla**.	Pensi che **lo squalo** stia imparando a volare?	**affilato, tagliente**	**L'affilatoio** serve ad affilare i coltelli.
2582 to share	2583 shark	2584 sharp	2585 knife sharpener
frantumare, rompere	**rasarsi, farsi la barba**	**le cesoie**	**l'affilatrice** per i pattini
2588 to shatter	2589 to shave	2590 shears	2586 skate sharpener
il fodero, la guaina	Sabrina conta **le pecore** per addormentarsi.	**il lenzuolo** del letto	**il temperamatite**
2591 sheath	2592 sheep	2593 sheet	2587 pencil sharpener
la mensola	**la conchiglia**	L'insetto ha trovato **un rifugio**.	**Il pastore** custodisce le pecore.
2594 shelf	2595 shell	2596 shelter	2597 shepherd
Lo scudo protegge il guerriero.	**lo stinco**	Il sole **risplende** nel cielo azzurro.	**l'assicella**
2598 shield	2599 shin	2600 to shine	2601 shingle

Il fuoco di Sant'Antonio è un male doloroso.	I diamanti della corona sono **splendenti**.	**la nave**	Robinson ha fatto **naufragio**.
2602 shingles	2603 shiny	2604 ship	2605 shipwreck
la camicia	**rabbrividire**	Attenzione alle **scosse** elettriche!	**le scarpe, le calzature**
2606 shirt	2607 to shiver	2608 shock	2609 shoes
Sei capace ad annodare **i legacci** delle scarpe?	**il calzolaio, il ciabattino**	**sparare, tirare**	**la bottega, il negozio**
2610 shoelace	2611 shoemaker	2612 to shoot	2613 shop
il bottegaio, il negoziante	**la vetrina**	**la spiaggia**	**piccolo** di statura
2614 shopkeeper	2615 shop window	2616 shore	2617 short
i calzoncini	**la spalla**	**urlare, strillare**	Non bisogna **urtare** la gente.
2618 shorts	2619 shoulder	2620 to shout	2621 to shove

la pala da neve

2622   shovel

mostrare

2623   to show

mettersi in mostra, pavoneggiarsi

2624   to show off

Finalmente **è comparso.**

2625   to show up/appear*

Remo sta facendo **la doccia.**

2626   shower

strillare, gridare

2627   to shriek

il gamberetto

2628   shrimp

La camicetta **si è accorciata.**

2629   to shrink

un arbusto, un cespuglio

2630   shrub

mescolare le carte

2631   shuffle

Di notte si chiudono **le imposte.**

2632   shutters

timido

2633   shy

ammalato

2634   sick

il fianco della casa

2635   side

Sabrina cammina sempre sul **marciapiede.**

2636   sidewalk/pavement*

sospirare di sollievo

2637   to sigh

il cartello

2638   sign

segnalare, fare segnali

2639   to signal

la firma

2640   signature

silenzioso

Non capita spesso che Sabrina sia **silenziosa.**
Una notte **silenziosa** è una notte tranquilla.

Sabrina is not silent very often.
A silent night is a quiet night.

2641   silent

il davanzale della finestra

2642   sill

sciocco, stupido

Gregorio pensa che Sabrina sia assolutamente **sciocca**. Sabrina pensa che Gregorio faccia cose **stupide**.

Gregorio thinks Sabrina is utterly silly.
Sabrina thinks Gregorio does silly things.

2643   silly

l'argento

2644   silver

semplice

E' la verità pura e **semplice**. C'è una soluzione molto **semplice**.

That is the pure and simple truth.
There is a very simple solution.

2645   simple

cantare

2646   to sing

singolare

'Uomo' è il **singolare** di 'uomini'.
'Uomo' è **singolare**, 'uomini' è plurale.

'Man' is the singular of 'men'.
'Man' is singular, 'men' is plural.

2647   singular

il lavandino della cucina

2648   sink

Aiuto! La barca **affonda**.

2649   to sink

centellinare, sorseggiare

2650   to sip

la sirena

2651   siren

Paola **è la sorella** di Osvaldo.

2652   sister

sedere, essere seduto

2653   to sit

sei

2654   six

la sesta

2655   sixth

Questo è della mia **taglia**!

2656   size

pattinare

2657   to skate

lo skateboard

2658   skateboard

Che cosa fa **uno scheletro** nel mio armadio?

2659   skeleton

L'artista **abbozza** una figura.

2660   to sketch

gli sci

2661   skis

sciare	**slittare**	**la pelle**	**saltare** alla corda
2662　to ski	2663　to skid	2664　skin	2665　to skip
Il capitano regge il timone.	**la gonna**	**il cranio**, **il teschio**	**Il cielo** è nuvoloso.
2666　skipper/captain*	2667　skirt	2668　skull	2669　sky
un'**allodola**	**il grattacielo**	**Ha sbattuto** la porta.	un pavimento **inclinato**
2670　skylark	2671　skyscraper	2672　to slam	2673　slanting floor
schiaffeggiare	Zorro ha ripreso a **sfregiare**.	**la lavagnetta**	**La slitta** scivola giù per la china.
2674　to slap	2675　to slash	2676　slate	2677　sled/sleigh*
Zorro che **dorme**	**il sacco a pelo**	Paolo è **assonnato**.	**il nevischio**
2678　to sleep	2679　sleeping bag	2680　sleepy	2681　sleet

la manica

2682   sleeve

lo scivolo

2683   slide

Una è **snella**, l'altra è grassa.

2684   slim

Il verme ha un corpo **viscido**.

2685   slimy

Ha il braccio al collo in **una benda**.

2686   sling

la fionda

2687   slingshot/catapult*

scivolare

2688   to slip

la pantofola

2689   slipper

viscido

2690   slippery

Quant' è **trascurato**!

2691   slob

il pendio del monte

2692   slope

la fessura

2693   slot

Il ragazzo cammina **dinoccolato**.

2694   to slouch

rallentare

Rallenta, papà! Vai troppo forte.
La macchina **rallenta** all'angolo della strada.

Slow down, Dad! You are going too fast.
The car slows down at the corner.

2695   to slow down

la poltiglia, la neve sciolta

2696   slush

Uno è **piccolo**, l'altro è grande.

2697   small

intelligente, elegante

Sabrina si crede molto **intelligente**, perché ha superato l'esame.
Ella indossa un abito molto **elegante**.

Sabrina thinks she is very smart because she passed her exam.
She is wearing a very smart dress.

2698   smart/clever*

Non **fracassare** l'orologio.

2699   to smash

imbrattare, macchiare

2700   to smear

Ernesto **odora** il fiore rosso.

2701   to smell

La puzzola emette un liquido **nauseabondo**.

2702   smelly

fumare

2703   to smoke

liscio, **senza scosse**

Il ghiaccio su cui Sabrina pattina è molto **liscio**.
Un buon pilota di aereo atterra **senza scosse**.

The ice Sabrina is skating on is very smooth.
A good airplane pilot makes smooth landings.

2704   smooth

A Noemi piace **fare spuntini** tra i pasti.

2705   to have a snack

la lumaca

2706   snail

il serpente

2707   snake

spezzarsi d'un colpo

2708   to snap

le scarpe da tennis

2709   sneakers/trainers*

starnutire

2710   to sneeze

la maschera e **il boccaglio**

2711   snorkel

La neve scende a larghe falde.

2712   snow

il fiocco di neve

2713   snowflake

le racchette da neve

2714   snowshoes

Lavati le mani col **sapone**.

2715   soap

il calcio

2716   soccer

il calzino

2717   sock

la presa di corrente

2718   socket

il divano, il sofà

2719   sofa/couch*

Batuffo ha il pelo **soffice**.

2720   soft

il soldato

2721   soldier

la sogliola
2722   sole

Ella **risolve** il problema.
2723   She **solves** the problem.

**fare un salto mortale,
fare una capriola**
2724   to **somersault**

il padre e **il figlio**
2725   son

il canto, la canzone
2726   song

presto, tra poco
Sarà **presto** notte.
Sabrina tornerà **tra poco**.

*Soon it will be dark.
Sabrina will be home soon.*
2727   soon

Il mago fa un incantesimo.
2728   sorcerer

Il mio braccio è **dolorante**.
2729   My arm is **sore.**

l'acetosella
2730   sorrel

Maciste è davvero
spiacente.
2731   sorry

Alfio **separa** le uova chiare
da quelle scure.
2732   to **sort**

la minestra, la zuppa
2733   soup

Il limone ha un sapore
agro.
2734   sour

il sud
2735   south

La scrofa è la madre dei
porcellini.
2736   sow

seminare
2737   to **sow**

la nave spaziale
2738   spaceship

La vanga serve per il
giardinaggio.
2739   spade

sculacciare
2740   to **spank**

la ruota di scorta
2741   spare tire/tyre*

la scintilla, la favilla

2742   spark

Gli anelli **scintillano** al sole.

2743   to sparkle

il passero

2744   sparrow

Che lingua **parlano**?

2745   to speak

la lancia

2746   spear

La tartaruga ha difficoltà ad **accelerare**.

2747   to speed up

Annalisa **scrive** il suo nome **lettera per lettera**.

2748   to spell

spendere del denaro

2749   to spend

La sfera è rotonda.

2750   sphere

piccante

2751   spicy

Il ragno tesse la sua ragnatela.

2752   spider

un aculeo

2753   spike

versare

2754   to spill

far girare

2755   to spin

gli spinaci

2756   spinach

la spina dorsale

2757   spine

la spirale

2758   spiral

la guglia del campanile

2759   spire

Sputare non è da persona educata.

2760   to spit

schizzare, sguazzare

2761   to splash

la scheggia di legno

2762   splinter

della frutta guasta

2763   spoiled/rotten* fruit

la spugna

2764   sponge

un rocchetto di filo

2765   spool/reel*

il cucchiaio

2766   spoon

Donde viene questa brutta **macchia**?

2767   spot

il beccuccio della teiera

2768   spout

prendere una storta, **slogarsi** una caviglia

2769   to sprain

spruzzare

2770   to spray

spalmare

2771   to spread

la molla

2772   spring

La primavera è arrivata.

2773   spring

spargere

2775   to sprinkle

scattare, fare una volata

2776   to sprint

l'abete rosso

2777   spruce

una sorgente d'acqua pura

2774   spring

il quadrato

2778   square

la zucca

2779   squash

accoccolarsi

2780   to squat

Sabrina **stringe** la sua amica tra le braccia.

2781   to squeeze

il calamaro	**lo scoiattolo**	**sprizzare**	**la stalla** per i cavalli
2782 squid	2783 squirrel	2784 to squirt	2785 stable

il palcoscenico del teatro	**la macchia, la chiazza**	Dove porta questa **scala**?	**un paletto** di legno
2786 stage	2787 stain	2788 staircase	2789 wooden stake

stantio	**un gambo** di sedano	**Lo stallone** è un cavallo maschio.	**il francobollo**
A Sabrina non piace il pane **stantio**; lo preferisce fresco. *Sabrina does not like stale bread; she prefers it fresh.*			
2790 **stale** bread	2791 celery **stalk**	2792 stallion	2793 stamp

essere in piedi	**la stella**	Sabrina **guarda fisso** davanti a sè.	**lo storno**
2794 to stand	2795 star	2796 to stare	2797 starling

avviare il motore dell'auto	**morire di fame, avere una fame da lupo**	**una stazione di servizio, un distributore** di benzina	**una stazione** ferroviara
	Quando Sabrina arriva da scuola, grida sempre: ''**Muoio di fame!**'' **Ha una fame da lupo**, ma non **muore** veramente **di fame**. *When Sabrina comes home from school, she always shouts: ''I am starving.'' She is very hungry but she will not really starve.*		
2798 to **start** a car	2799 to **starve**	2800 gas/petrol* station	2801 train/railway* station

la statua

2802   statue

Midoro ! **Sta** li **fermo !**

2803   **Stay** there!

la bistecca

2804   steak

rubare

2805   to **steal**

il vapore

2806   steam

I coltelli sono fatti d'**acciaio**.

2807   Kinves are made of **steel**.

ripido

2808   steep

il manzo

2809   steer/bullock*

lo stelo della rosa

2811   stem

il gradino

2812   step

E' **entrata** in una pozzanghera.

2813   to **step** in

sterzare

2810   to **steer**

Papà ha preparato **lo stufato**.

2815   stew

il rametto

2816   stick

uscire per un minuto

2814   to **step** out

Armando ha le mani **appiccicose**.

2817   sticky

rigido, duro

Lo zio Giovanni ha una gamba **rigida**.
Questo spazzolino da denti è troppo **duro**.

*Uncle Giovanni has a stiff leg.
This toothbrush is too stiff.*

2818   stiff

Un'ape l'**ha punta**.

2819   to **sting**

la puntura dell'ape

2820   sting

puzzare

2821   to **stink**

Mescolare prima di bere.

2822   to stir

le calze

2823   stockings

caricare una caldaia

2824   to stoke

lo stomaco

2825   stomach

Tirare **sassi** è pericoloso.

2826   stone

lo sgabello

2827   stool

Si china per raccogliere la palla.

2828   to stoop/bend down*

lo stop, **il segnale di stop**

2829   stop

il negozio

2832   store/shop*

la cicogna

2833   stork

il temporale, **un uragano**

2834   storm

Riesce a **fermare** il treno.

2830   He **stops** the train.

Zia Anna legge **una storia**.

2835   story

la cucina elettrica

2836   stove/cooker*

diritto

2837   straight

L'aereo ha fatto **uno scalo**.

2831   to **stop over**

colare, filtrare

2838   to strain

sforzare, affaticare

2839   to strain

un animaletto **strano**

2840   strange

Lo scimmione lo vuole **strangolare**.

2841   to **strangle**

la bretella

2842   strap

Ti piace sorbire la bibita con **la cannuccia**?

2843   straw

la fragola

2844   strawberry

il corso d'acqua, il ruscello

2845   stream

la bandierina

2846   streamer/pennant*

La strada è deserta.

2847   street

il lampione

2848   street light/lamp*

estendere

2849   to stretch

la barella

2850   stretcher

lo sciopero

Gli operai sono in **sciopero**. Fanno **sciopero** per ottenere più denaro.

The workers are on strike. They strike for more money.

2851   strike

Non bisogna **picchiare** la gente.

2852   to strike

Lo spago è avvolto sul rocchetto.

2853   string

un asciugamano a **strisce**

2854   stripe

E' molto **forte**.

2855   strong

lo scolaro

2856   student

Pino **studia** assiduamente.

2857   to study

un animale **imbottito**

2858   a **stuffed** animal

il ceppo di un albero

2859   stump

Il sottomarino naviga sott'acqua.

2860   submarine

sottrarre

5-2:3

2861   to subtract

succhiare
2862   to suck

improvvisamente, ad un tratto
Albina andò via **improvvisamente**.
Tutto **ad un tratto** cominciò a piovere.

*Albina left suddenly.
Suddenly, it began to rain.*

2863   suddenly

Non mangiare troppo **zucchero**.

2864   sugar

Luigi porta **un abito completo**.

2865   suit

la valigia
2866   suitcase

la scorsa **estate** al mare

2867   summer

il sole
2868   sun

domenica
La domenica è il settimo giorno della settimana.
Ogni **domenica** la mamma fa un dolce.

*Sunday is the seventh day of the week.
Every Sunday, Mother bakes a cake.*

2869   Sunday

La meridiana segna le ore.

2870   sundial

Il girasole guarda sempre il sole.

2871   sunflower

il levar del sole

2872   sunrise

il tramonto del sole

2873   sunset

La signora Ida fa la spesa al **supermercato**.

2874   supermarket

la cena
2875   supper/dinner*

sicuro, certo
Questo è un modo **sicuro** per vincere.
Sono **certo** che domani farà bello.

*That is a sure way to win.
I am sure it will be nice tomorrow.*

2876   sure

la superficie
2877   surface

il chirurgo
2878   surgeon

il cognome
Il mio nome è Sabrina; **il** mio **cognome** è Borello.

My first name is Sabrina; my surname is Borello.

2879   surname

una festa **a sorpresa, inattesa**

2880   surprise party

Non sparate! **Mi arrendo!**

2881   to surrender

circondare, attorniare

2882   to **surround**

Le bretelle servono a tenere su i pantaloni.

2883   suspenders/braces*

inghiottire, ingoiare

2884   to **swallow**

Il cigno è maestoso.

2885   swan

scambiare

2886   to **swap**

uno sciame di api

2887   swarm

sudare a profusione

2888   to **sweat**

il maglione

2889   sweater/sweatshirt*

scopare

2890   to **sweep**

dolce

2891   sweet

Per fortuna l'auto **ha deviato.**

2892   to **swerve**

Lucia **nuota** molto bene.

2893   to **swim**

l'altalena

2894   swing

dondolare

2895   to **swing**

un interruttore

2896   switch

accendere, spegnere

Accendi la luce, per favore. E' meglio **spegnere** il televisore.

Switch on the light, please. It is best to switch off the television.

2897   to **switch**

piombare sulla preda

2898   to **swoop**

la spada

2899   sword

il sicomoro

2900   sycamore

Lo sciroppo d'acero si mette sulle cialde calde.

2901   syrup

la tavola, il tavolo

2902   table

la tovaglia

2903   tablecloth

la compressa, la pillola

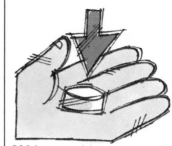

2904   tablet

la bulletta

2905   tack

affrontare, contrastare

Sabrina deve **affrontare** la questione al più presto.
Aldo **contrastò** Giuseppe durante la partita di football.

Sabrina must tackle that problem as soon as possible. Aldo tackled Giuseppe during the football game.

2906   to tackle

Il **girino** diventerà una rana.

2907   tadpole

la coda

2908   tail

prendere

2910   to take

smontare

2911   to take apart

estrarre

2912   to take away

riportare, portare indietro

2913   to take back

togliere, togliersi

2914   to take off

decollare

2915   to take off

portare fuori

2916   to take out

Lucilla **ritira** il pollo arrosto per la famiglia.

2917   take-out/take-away*

Il **sarto** confeziona vestiti.

2909   tailor

la favola, la storia

2918   tale

il talento

Sabrina ha un grande **talento** per la danza.
La danza classica richiede sia **il talento** che l'esercizio continuo.

Sabrina has a great talent for dancing. Dance requires both talent and hard work.

2919   talent

parlare

2920   to talk

alto di statura	**il tamburello**	I leoni da circo sono **addomesticati**.	Erica ha **una** bella **abbronzatura**.
2921 tall	2922 tambourine	2923 tame	2924 tan
il mandarino	Il filo si è **ingarbugliato**.	**la cisterna, il serbatoio**	**la petroliera, la nave cisterna**
2925 tangerine	2926 tangled	2927 tank	2928 tanker
Il **rubinetto** non chiude bene.	**il nastro** adesivo	**fissare col nastro adesivo**	**il registratore, il magnetofono**
2929 tap	2930 tape	2931 to tape	2932 tape recorder
il catrame	Ha colpito **il bersaglio** in pieno.	**il targone**	**la pasta**
2933 tar	2934 target	2935 tarragon	2936 tart
Il suo **incarico** è di scopare il pavimento.	**Assaggia** e dimmi se ti piace.	**gustoso, saporito** E' stata una cena veramente **gustosa**. Questa salsa è molto **saporita**. *That was a tasty meal.* *This sauce is really tasty.*	**il tassì**
2937 task	2938 to taste	2939 tasty	2940 taxi

una tazza di **tè**

2941   a cup of tea

La signorina Perfetti **insegna** l'aritmetica.

2942   to teach

E' la nostra **insegnante**.

2943   teacher

una squadra affiatata

2944   team

la teiera

2945   teapot

la lacrima

2946   tear

stracciare

2947   to tear

Non bisogna **strappare via** le pagine dai quaderni.

2948   to tear out

il telegramma

2949   telegram

il telefono

2950   telephone

telefonare

2951   to telephone

Il telescopio è puntato verso il cielo.

2952   telescope

Il televisore è anche chiamato "la TV".

2953   television

dire

2954   to tell

temperamento

Nicola ha un pessimo **temperamento**.
Non riesce a controllare il suo **temperamento**.

Nicola has a bad temper.
He cannot control his temper.

2955   temper

Il termometro segna **la temperatura**.

2956   temperature

dieci mele

2957   ten apples

una racchetta e una palla da **tennis**

2958   tennis racquet and ball

una scarpa **da tennis**

2959   tennis shoe

Sabrina ha dormito sotto **la tenda**.

2960   tent

La decima lumaca è verde.

2961   tenth

il terminal del calcolatore elettronico

2962   terminal

provare la temperatura dell'acqua

2963   to **test** the water

Lei lo **ringrazia** di tutto cuore.

2964   to thank

sgelare, fondere

2965   to thaw

il teatro

2966   theater/theatre*

La palla è **là**.

2967   there

Il termometro è graduato.

2968   thermometer

Quest'albero ha un tronco molto **grosso**.

2969   thick

Ladro oggi . . . . . . galeotto domani!

2970   thief

la coscia

2971   thigh

il ditale per cucire

2972   thimble

Questo è **sottile**.

2973   thin

la cosa

Una persona non è **una cosa**. Sabrina dice molte **cose** divertenti.

A person is not a thing. Sabrina says many funny things.

2974   thing

pensare

2975   to think

la terza lumaca

2976   third

assetato

2977   thirsty

Sta attenta! **Il cardo** punge.

2978   thistle

Anche **la spina** punge.

2979   thorn

il filo

2980   thread

Sei capace di **infilare** il filo nell'ago?

2981   to thread

tre mele

2982   three

la soglia della porta

2983   threshold

la gola

2984   throat

il trono della regina

2985   throne

lanciare, **gettare**

2986   to throw

Vomita perché soffre il mal di mare.

2987 to throw up/be sick*

il pollice

2988   thumb

un tuono assordante

2989   thunder

il temporale

2990   thunderstorm

giovedì

Giovedì è il quarto giorno della settimana.
Sabrina prende lezioni di nuoto al **giovedì**.

*Thursday is the fourth day of the week.
Sabrina has a swimming class on Thursdays.*

2991   Thursday

Il timo insaporisce l'arrosto.

2992   thyme

il biglietto della ferrovia

2993   ticket

fare il solletico, **solleticare**

2994   to tickle

ordinato, **pulito**

2995   tidy

Mi annodo **la cravatta** da solo.

2996   tie

La tigre va a caccia.

2998   tiger

stringere la cintura

2999   to tighten

le piastrelle, **le mattonelle**

3000   tiles

legare, **annodare**

2997   to tie

La barca **si inclina** pericolosamente.

3001   to **tilt**

Che **ora** è?

3002   What **time** is it?

minuscola

3003   tiny

La barca **si è rovesciata**.

3004   to **tip**

camminare in punta di piedi

3006   tiptoe

un vecchio pneumatico

3007   tire/tyre*

stanco, affaticato

3008   tired

dare la mancia

3005   to **tip**

Il rospo vive nello stagno.

3009   toad

il pane tostato, il crostino

3010   toast

il tostapane

3011   toaster

oggi

La scuola comincia **oggi**.
Oggi Sabrina si alza presto a preparare la colazione.

School starts today.
Today, Sabrina gets up early to prepare breakfast.

3012   today

le dita dei piedi

3013   toes

Siamo seduti **insieme**.

3014   We are sitting **together**.

il gabinetto

3015   toilet

il pomodoro

3016   tomato

la tomba

3017   tomb

domani

Oggi verrà seguito da **domani**.
Domani Sabrina andrà a vedere i dinosauri al museo.

Today is followed by tomorrow.
Tomorrow Sabrina is going to see dinosaurs at the museum.

3018   tomorrow

le pinze, le molle

3019   tongs

Non mostrare **la lingua**!

3020   tongue

Pesa **una tonnellata**.

3021   It weighs a **ton**.

le tonsille

3022   tonsils

gli arnesi da lavoro

3023   tools

Ha **i denti** belli perché se li lava spesso.

3024   tooth

il mal di denti

3025   toothache

lo spazzolino da denti

3026   toothbrush

il dentifricio

3027   toothpaste

la parte superiore

3028   top

I cubi **ruzzolano giù**.

3030   to **topple**

la fiaccola olimpica

3031   torch

La tromba d'aria distrugge tutto al suo passaggio.

3032   tornado

La trottola gira.

3029   top

il torrente

3033   torrent

la tartaruga

3034   tortoise

Robi le **lancia** la palla.

3035   to **toss**

toccare

3036   to **touch**

Sono un **duro**.

3037   I am **tough**.

Il carro attrezzi **rimorchia** l'auto.

3038   to **tow**

L'asciugamano di Sabrina è bagnato.

3039   towel

la torre più alta del mondo

3040   tower

La casa di Sabrina è nei pressi di questa **città**.

3041   town

Raccogli **i** tuoi **giocattoli**, per favore!

3042   toys

tracciare

3043   to trace

Il treno corre sui **binari**.

3044   track

il trattore

3045   tractor

scambiare, commerciare

3046   to trade

Il traffico è intenso.

3047   traffic

il semaforo

3048   traffic light

Segue **una** buona **pista**.

3049   trail

Che cosa trasporta questo **rimorchio**?

3050   trailer

il treno

3051   train

Addestra il cane.

3052   to train

il vagabondo

3053   tramp

Non **calpestate** i fiori!

3054   to trample

il trampolino

3055   trampoline

La mamma di Marisa non è **trasparente**.

3056   transparent

trasportare

3057   to transport

l'autocarro

3058   transporter/lorry*

la trappola

3059   trap

il trapezio

3060   trapeze

Zia Rosmunda **viaggia** in treno.

3061 to travel

Remo porta **il vassoio** delle bibite.

3062 tray

il battistrada del pneumatico

3063 tread

il tesoro

3064 treasure

un albero

3065 tree

Monica **trema** dalla paura.

3066 to tremble

il fosso

3067 trench

il processo

3068 trial

Il triangolo ha tre lati.

3069 triangle

il trucco, **l'artificio**

3070 trick

L'acqua **gocciola** lentamente.

3071 to trickle

Il triciclo ha tre ruote.

3072 tricycle

il grilletto della pistola

3073 trigger

La pettinatrice le **spunta** i capelli.

3074 to trim

un viaggio breve

3075 a short **trip**

inciampare

3076 to trip

il filobus

3077 trolley bus

Ai puledri piace **trottare** e galoppare.

3078 to trot

il trogolo dei maiali

3079 trough

i pantaloni

3080 trousers

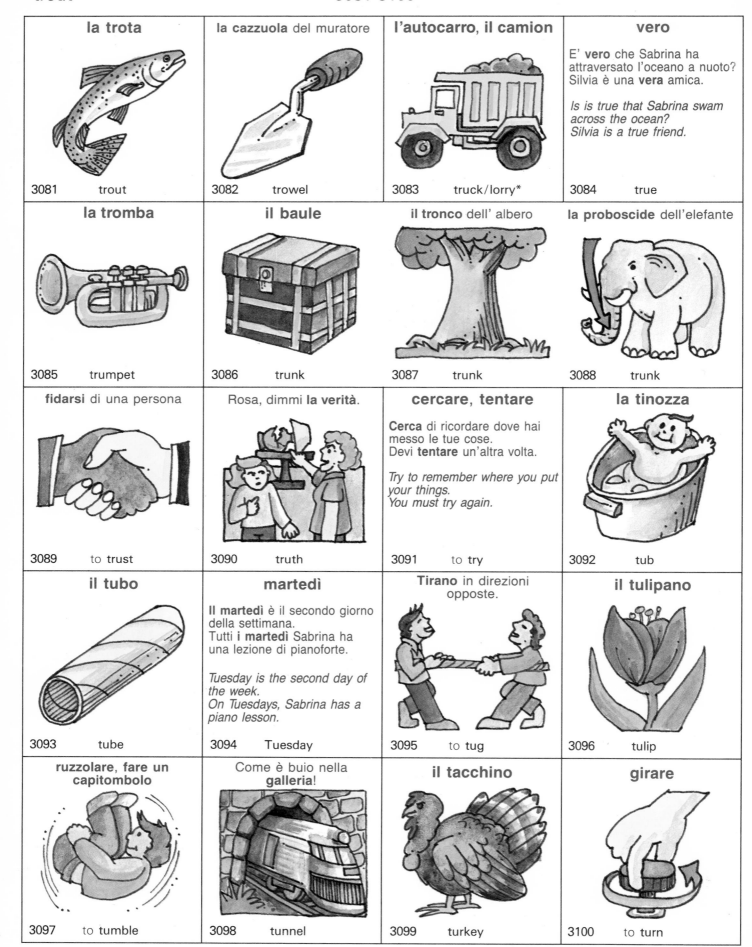

la trota
3081   trout

la cazzuola del muratore
3082   trowel

l'autocarro, il camion
3083   truck/lorry*

vero
E' **vero** che Sabrina ha attraversato l'oceano a nuoto?
Silvia è una **vera** amica.

Is is true that Sabrina swam across the ocean?
Silvia is a true friend.

3084   true

la tromba
3085   trumpet

il baule
3086   trunk

il tronco dell' albero
3087   trunk

la proboscide dell'elefante
3088   trunk

fidarsi di una persona
3089   to trust

Rosa, dimmi la verità.
3090   truth

cercare, tentare
Cerca di ricordare dove hai messo le tue cose.
Devi **tentare** un'altra volta.

Try to remember where you put your things.
You must try again.

3091   to try

la tinozza
3092   tub

il tubo
3093   tube

martedì
Il martedì è il secondo giorno della settimana.
Tutti **i martedì** Sabrina ha una lezione di pianoforte.

Tuesday is the second day of the week.
On Tuesdays, Sabrina has a piano lesson.

3094   Tuesday

Tirano in direzioni opposte.
3095   to tug

il tulipano
3096   tulip

ruzzolare, fare un capitombolo
3097   to tumble

Come è buio nella galleria!
3098   tunnel

il tacchino
3099   turkey

girare
3100   to turn

spegnere la luce

3101   to turn off

accendere la luce

3102   to turn on

diventare, riuscire

Carletto **è diventato** un vero discolo.
Tutto **è riuscito** bene.

*Carletto turned out a real brat.
Things turned out well.*

3103   to turn out

Silvia **gira** la bistecca.

3104   to turn over

la rapa

3105   turnip

il giradischi

3106   turntable

turchese

3107   turquoise

Sulla **torretta** sventola la bandiera rossa.

3108   turret

la tartaruga

3109   turtle

Le zanne dell'elefante sono d'avorio.

3110   tusk

le pinzette

3111   tweezers

due volte, il doppio

Sabrina è andata **due volte** allo zoo.
Carla ha **il doppio** dei libri di Sabrina.

*Sabrina has been to the zoo twice.
Carla has twice as many books as Sabrina.*

3112   twice

il rametto

3113   twig

I gemelli sono identici.

3114   twins

Le stelle **scintillano**.

3115   Stars twinkle.

far girare, mulinare

3116   to twirl

torcere

3117   to twist

due

3118   two

scrivere a macchina, dattilografare

3119   to type

la macchina da scrivere

3120   typewriter

E' brutta, ma è molto gentile.

3121   ugly

l'ombrello

3122   umbrella

lo zio

Mio **zio** è il fratello di mia madre.
L'altro mio **zio** è fratello di mio padre.

My uncle is my mother's brother.
My other uncle is my father's brother.

3123   uncle

sotto

Sabrina si è nascosta **sotto** le coperte.
I bambini **sotto** i 5 anni non possono andarvi.

Sabrina is hiding under the covers.
Children under 5 cannot go.

3124   under

comprendere

3125   to understand

la biancheria intima

3126   underwear

svestirsi

3127   to undress

infelice, scontenta

3128   unhappy

L'unicorno esiste solo nelle favole.

3129   unicorn

Zio Riccardo porta **l'uniforme**.

3130   uniform

un'università

3131   university

Che cosa **sta scaricando** l'autocarro?

3132   to unload

aprire con la chiave

3133   to unlock

aprire un pacco, scartocciare

3134   to unwrap

in piedi

3135   upright

capovolto, sottosopra

3136   upside-down

Mamma **usa** il pepe in cucina.

3137   to use

Ha **esaurito** il pepe.

3138   to use up

Questo temperino è molto **utile**.

3139   useful

Viva **le vacanze!**

3140   vacation/holiday*

il vapore

3141   vapor/vapour*

Vernicia il legno per proteggerlo.

3142   to **varnish**

Sabrina ha regalato **un vaso** alla mamma.

3143   vase

una bistecca di **vitello**

3144   veal

la verdura

3145   vegetable

il veicolo

3146   vehicle

---

la veletta, il velo

3147   veil

la vena

3148   vein

il veleno

Certi serpenti producono del **veleno**.
Anche alcuni insetti hanno **il veleno**.

Some snakes produce venom.
Some insects also have venom.

3149   venom

Una linea verticale va diritta dall'alto in basso.

3150   vertical

---

molto, proprio

Sabrina pensa che suo fratello sia **molto** furbo.
Te l'ha fatta **proprio** sotto gli occhi.

Sabrina thinks her little brother is very clever.
He did it under your very eyes.

3151   very

il panciotto

3152   vest/waistcoat*

Il veterinario cura gli animali.

3153   veterinarian/veterinary surgeon*

la vittima del delitto

3154   victim

---

il video registratore

3155   video recorder

Non bisogna giocare con **il nastro della videocassetta**.

3156   video tape

il panorama, la veduta

Che bel **panorama**, dalla cima della montagna!
Ciascuno di noi ha **le** proprie **vedute**.

What a wonderful view from the top of the mountain!
We each have our own point of view.

3157   view

il villaggio, il paese

3158   village

il furfante, il mascalzone

3159 villain

La vite produce i grappoli d'uva.

3160 vine

A Sabrina piace mettere **l'aceto** sulle patatine.

3161 vinegar

Alla nonna piace il profumo delle **violette**.

3162 violet

il violino

3163 violin

Per entrare in certi paesi occorre **un visto**.

3164 visa

visibile

Ci sono molte nuvole questa sera e le stelle sono appena **visibili**.
Un uomo invisibile non è **visibile** per nulla.

There are many clouds tonight and the stars are barely visible. An invisible man cannot be seen.

3165 visible

Lorenzo **visita** sua zia, che è ammalata.

3166 to visit

la visiera

3167 visor

il vocabolario

Sabrina ha **un** buon **vocabolario**; conosce molte parole.
Questo dizionario vi aiuterà ad aumentare **il** vostro **vocabolario**.

Sabrina has a good vocabulary; she knows many words. This dictionary will help increase your vocabulary.

3168 vocabulary

la voce

3169 voice

Il vulcano è in eruzione.

3170 volcano

la pallovolo

3171 volleyball

La volontaria aiuta la signora Bea.

3172 volunteer

vomitare

3173 to vomit

votare

3174 to vote

un elettore

3175 voter

la vocale

A,E,I,O,U sono **le vocali** dell'alfabeto italiano.

A, E, I, O, U are the vowels of the Italian alphabet.

3176 vowel

la traversata

3177 voyage

un avvoltoio

3178 vulture

guadare

3179   to wade

la cialda

3180   waffle

Il cavallo tira **il carro**.

3181   wagon/cart*

gemere, lamentarsi

3182   to wail

Debora ha **la vita** sottile.

3183   waist

Carmela **aspetta** l'autobus.

3184   to wait

La mamma **sveglia** Golia.

3185   to wake

Cammina a grandi passi.

3186   to walk

il muro

3187   wall

il portafogli

3188   wallet

la noce

3189   walnut

il tricheco

3190   walrus

la bacchetta magica

3191   wand

vagare

3192   to wander

volere

Papà **vuole** che Sabrina lo aiuti a lavare i piatti.
Ella lo **vorrebbe** aiutare, ma non c'è acqua.

*Dad wants Sabrina to help him wash the dishes.
She wants to help him but there is no water.*

3193   to want

Sabrina odia **la guerra**.

3194   war

il corredo

3195   wardrobe

il magazzino

3196   warehouse

un maglione bello **caldo**

3197   warm

Vieni a **scaldarti** vicino al fuoco.

3198   to **warm** up

avvertire, ammonire

3199   to **warn**

la garenna, la conigliera

3200   **warren**

Il guerriero ha sfoderato la spada.

3201   **warrior**

la verruca

3202   **wart**

lavare

3203   to **wash** up

la lavatrice

3204   **washing** machine

il bagno

3205   **washroom/toilet***

Sabrina è stata punta da **una vespa**.

3206   **wasp**

Non bisogna **sprecare** il cibo.

3207   to **waste**

un orologio

3208   **watch**

Sorveglia i pesci rossi attentamente.

3209   to **watch**

l'acqua

3210   **water**

un annaffiatoio

3211   **watering** can

Il crescione vive nell'acqua.

3212   **watercress**

la cascata

3213   **waterfall**

l'anguria

3214   **watermelon**

impermeabile

3215   **waterproof**

lo sci nautico

3216   **waterskiing**

un'onda

3217   **wave**

Katia fa **un cenno** con la mano a Luigi.

3218   to wave

Ha i capelli **ondulati**.

3219   wavy

La cera della candela cola.

3220   wax

Uno è **debole**, l'altro è forte.

3221   weak

un'arma pericolosa

3222   weapon

Indossa un cappotto pesante.

3223   to wear

la donnola

3224   weasel

Che **tempo** fa?

3225   weather

intrecciare

3226   to weave

un piede palmato

3227   web foot

lo sposalizio, le nozze

3228   wedding

il cuneo, lo spicchio

3229   wedge

mercoledì

Mercoledì è il terzo giorno della settimana.
Al mercoledì Sabrina porta fuori i rifiuti.

Wednesday is the third day of the week.
On Wednesdays, Sabrina takes out the garbage.

3230   Wednesday

Il giardino è stato invaso dalle **erbacce**.

3231   weed

la settimana

3232   week

il fine settimana, il weekend

Il fine settimana comprende il sabato e la domenica.
Zia Lucia ci farà visita questo **weekend**.

Saturday and Sunday make a weekend.
Aunt Lucie will visit us this weekend.

3233   weekend

Piange perché è triste.

3234   to weep

pesare

3235   to weigh

Questa figura è **bizzarra**.

3236   weird

dare il benvenuto

3237   to welcome

Non cadere nel **pozzo**!

3238 well

Mi sento **bene**.

3239 I feel **well**.

L'ovest è opposto all'est.

3240 west

bagnato, fradicio

3241 wet

la balena

3243 whale

il molo

3244 wharf

cosa, che cosa

Cosa è successo al pelo di Tigre?
Sabrina, **che cosa** hai fatto al gatto?

What has happened to the Tiger's fur?
Sabrina, what did you do to your cat?

3245 what

inzuppare

3242 to wet

Il grano serve a fare il pane.

3246 wheat

la ruota

3247 wheel

la carriola

3248 wheelbarrow

la sedia a rotelle

3249 wheelchair

quando

Quando verrà zia Emilia a trovarci, papà?
Quando verrà in vacanza.

When is Aunt Emilia coming to see us?
When she takes her holidays.

3250 when

dove

Ci siamo persi e la mamma non sa **dove** siamo.
So **dove** è, ma non riesco a trovarlo.

We are lost and Mom has no idea where we are.
I know where it is but I cannot find it.

3251 where

Non sa **quale** scegliere.

3252 which one

frignare, piagnucolare

3253 to whine

la frusta

3254 whip

il caprimulgo

3255 whippoorwill

Il frullino serve a montare la panna.

3256 whisk

i baffi del gatto

3257 whisker

Che cosa le **sussurra** all'orecchio?	**il fischietto**	**fischiare**	**bianco**
3258 to whisper	3259 whistle	3260 to whistle	3261 white
Chi ci va?	**perché** Voglio sapere **perché** Sabrina ha preso la mia cravatta. **Perché** non riesce a ricordarsene? *I want to know why Sabrina took my tie.* *Why can she not remember?*	**Lo stoppino** brucia lentamente.	**malvagio, perfido**
3262 Who is going?	3263 why	3264 wick	3265 wicked
più **larga** che lunga	**la moglie** del signor Paolo	Il leone è un animale **selvaggio**.	**Il salice** ha lunghi rami.
3266 wide	3267 wife	3268 The lion is a **wild** animal.	3269 willow
I fiori **appassiscono** quando non sono innaffiati.	**astuto, scaltro**	**vincere**	Luigi **trasalì** per il dolore.
3270 to wilt	3271 wily	3272 to win	3273 to wince
Il vento soffia furiosamente.	**caricare** un orologio	**giacca a vento**	**Il mulino a vento** ha lunghe pale.
3274 wind	3275 to wind	3276 windbreaker	3277 windmill

la finestra	**il parabrezza**	**Il vino** è una bevanda per adulti.	**un'ala**
3278 window	3279 windshield/windscreen*	3280 wine	3281 wing
ammiccare, strizzare l'occhio	Ti piace **l'inverno**?	**Strofinalo** bene, per favore.	Gli uccelli sono appollaiati sui **fili**.
3282 to wink	3283 winter	3284 to wipe	3285 wire
saggio, prudente Il nonno è un vecchio **saggio**. Sabrina, pensi che sia **prudente** camminare nel bosco da sola? *Grandfather is a wise old man. Sabrina, do you think it is wise to walk in the forest alone?*	formulare **un desiderio**	**la strega**	**il mago**
3286 wise	3287 to make a wish	3288 witch	3289 wizard
il lupo	**la donna**	**chiedersi, meravigliarsi**	**meraviglioso**
3290 wolf	3291 woman	3292 to wonder	3293 wonderful
la legna da ardere	**Il picchio** scava i tronchi degli alberi.	Passeggiano nei **boschi**.	**la falegnameria**
3294 wood	3295 woodpecker	3296 woods	3297 woodwork

Lavora a maglia con **la lana**.

3298   wool

Che **parola** strana!

GLÜRP

3299   word

Un tipo di **lavoro**.

3300   work

Lavora in giardino.

3301   to work

l'officina

3303   workshop

il mondo

3304   world

Il verme striscia.

3305   worm

fare ginnastica

3302   to work out

La mamma **si preoccupa** per Sabrina.

3306   to worry

la ferita

3307   wound

avviluppare, incartare

3308   to wrap

la ghirlanda, la corona di fiori

3309   wreath

il relitto

3310   wreck

lo scricciolo

3311   wren

Lottano strenuamente.

3312   to wrestle

torcere, strizzare

3313   to wring

il polso

3314   wrist

un orologio da polso

3315   wristwatch

scrivere

3316   to write

male, sbagliato

E' **male** copiare e mentire. Penso che il nostro autobus stia andando nella direzione **sbagliata**.

It is wrong to cheat and to lie. I think our bus is going the wrong way.

3317   wrong

	i raggi x, la radiografia	**lo xilofono**	**un piccolo panfilo**
	3318 X-ray	3319 xylophone	3320 yacht

il giardino, la corte

Sbadiglia dalla noia o dal sonno?

un altro anno

gridare, urlare

3321   yard/garden*
3322   to yawn
3323   year
3324   to yell

giallo

sì

E' **sì**, è no, oppure è forse?
Se dici di **sì**, devi essere ben sicuro.

Is it yes, is it no, or is it maybe?
If you say yes, you had better be sure.

ieri

Ieri Sabrina non stava bene, perché aveva mangiato troppo gelato.
Che cosa hai fatto **ieri**?

Yesterday Sabrina was sick from eating too much ice cream.
What did you do yesterday?

Deve **cedere** il passo.

3325   yellow
3326   yes
3327   yesterday
3328   to yield/give way*

il tuorlo dell'uovo

giovane e vecchio

la zebra disegnata da Sabrina

lo zero

3329   yolk
3330   young
3331   zebra
3332   zero

la chiusura lampo

lo zoo

sfrecciare

Gli zucchini sono l'ultima parola di Sabrina.

3333   zipper/zip*
3334   zoo
3335   to zoom
3336   zucchini/courgette*

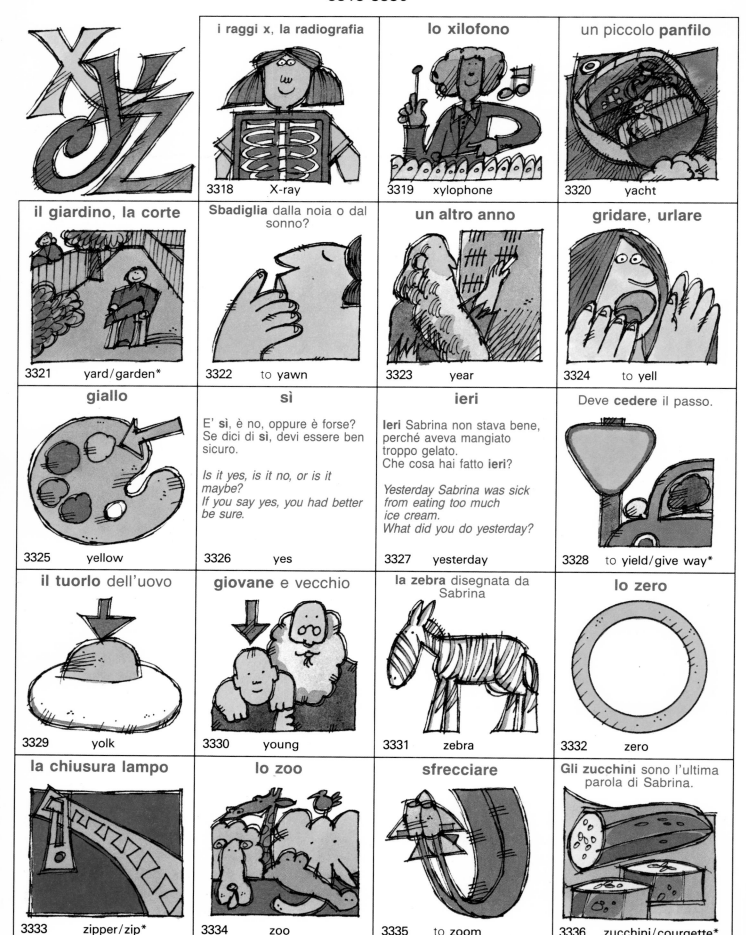

a

g

interno (il) 1434
interruttore (il) 2896
intervista (la) 1454
intonacare 2148
intonaco (il) 2147
ïntrecciare 3226
invadere 1457
invalido 1458
invece di 1449
inventare 1459
inverno (il) 3283
investigatore (il) 755
investire 2477
invisibile 1460
invitare 1462
invito (il) 1461
inzuppare 3242
ippopotamo (il) 1337
iris (il) 1463
iscriversi 2387
isola (la) 1467
isolamento (il) 1452
isolato (il) 281
ispettore (il) 1448
ispezionare 1447
istrice (il) 1301
istruttore (il) 1451
istruzione (la) 1450

j

jeans (i) 1482
jeep (la) 1483

k

kilt (il) 1527
kiwi (il) 1539
koala (il) 1549

l

là 2967
labbro (il) 1659

labirinto (il) 1755
laboratorio (il) 1551
lacerare 2430
lacerazione (la) 2535
lacrima (la) 2946
ladro (il) 2440, 2970
lago (il) 1560
lama (la) 265
lamentarsi 1208, 3182
lampada (la) 214, 1563
lampada elettrica (la) 1017
lampadina (la) 1639
lampione (il) 1564, 2848
lampo (il) 1016, 1642
lampone (il) 2347
lana (la) 3298
lancia (la) 1565, 2746
lanciare 1403, 1586, 2986, 3035
lanciare la palla 2132
lancio (il) 2133
lanterna (la) 1572
lanuggine (la) 1657
lanugine (la) 1034
lardo (il) 1575
largo 3266
larice (il) 1574
larva (la) 1710
lasciar cadere 836
lasciare 838, 1605, 1621
latte (il) 1793
lattina (la) 417
lattuga (la) 1624
lavagna (la) 262
lavagnetta (la) 2676
lavanda (la) 1590
lavanderia a secco (la) 844
lavandino (il) 2648
lavare 2541, 3203
lavatrice (la) 3204
lavorare 3301
lavorare a maglia 1543
lavorato 2139
lavoro (il) 1490, 3300
lecca-lecca (il) 1683
leccare 1630
legaccio (il) 2610
legare 250, 2997

legge (la) 1591
leggenda (la) 1612
leggere 2358
legna (la) 3294
legname da costruzione (il) 1704
legno compensato (il) 2171
lente (la) 1616, 1715
lentiggine (la) 1067
lenzuolo (il) 2593
leone (il) 1658
leopardo (il) 1617
lepre (la) 1269
lettera (la) 1622, 1623
lettino per bimbi (il) 669
letto (il) 213
leva (la) 1626
levar del sole (il) 2872
levigare 2187
lezione (la) 1620
libbra (la) 2217
libellula (la) 814
liberare 2394
liberarsi 1132
libero 1068
libro (il) 305
lillà (il) 1646
limare 985
limite (il) 1650
limonata (la) 1614
limone (il) 1613
lindo 1882
linea (la) 1652
linfa (la) 2501
lingua (la) 1571, 3020
lingua di gatto (la) 1558
liquido (il) 1035, 1661
liscio 1019, 2704
lista (la) 1662
litro (il) 1664
livido (il) 361
locomotiva (la) 1678
lontano 955
lontra (la) 1969
lottare 3312
lozione (la) 1691
lucchetto (il) 1992
luce (la) 1637

lucertola (la) 1670
lucidare 2187
luglio (il) 1499
lumaca (la) 2706
luna (la) 1832
lunedì (il) 1823
lungo 52, 1685
lupo (il) 3290

m

ma 393
macchiare 2700
macchia (la) 287, 2767, 2787
macchina (la) 436
macchina da cucire (la) 2574
macchina da scrivere (la) 3120
macchina dei pompieri (la) 998
macchina fotografica (la) 414
macchinista (il) 897
macellaio (il) 394
macinare 1206
madre (la) 1839
magazzino (il) 3196
maggio (il) 1752
magia (la) 1711
maglio (il) 1722
maglione (il) 2279, 2889
magnetofono (il) 2932
magnifico 1196, 1714
mago (il) 1712, 2728, 3289
mai 1901
maiale (il) 2113
maiuscolo 433
mal di denti (il) 3025
mal di testa (il) 1288
malato 1425
malattia (la) 782
male 3317
maleducato 2469
malvagio 3265
mamma (la) 1839

scaricare 851, 3132
scarico (lo) 815
scarlatto 2522
scarpa (la) 2609
scarpa da tennis (la) 2709
scartocciare 3134
scassinare 339
scassinatore (lo) 385
scatola (la) 325, 451
scattare 2776
scegliere 524, 2102
scena (la) 2523
scendere 1130, 1158
scheggia (la) 517, 2762
scheletro (lo) 2659
scherzo (lo) 1495
schiaccianoci (lo) 1925
schiacciare le patate
    1742
schiaffeggiare 2674
schiantarsi 659
schiena (la) 142
schiudere 1277
schiuma (la) 1039
schiuma di sapone (la)
    1583
schizzare 2761
sci (gli) 2661
sci nautico (lo) 3216
sciacquare 2428
scialuppa (la) 1585
scialuppa di salvataggio
    (la) 1635
sciame (lo) 2887
sciare 2662
sciarpa (la) 2521
scimmia (la) 79, 1825
scimpanzè (lo) 514
scintilla (la) 2742
scintillare 2743, 3115
sciocco 2643
sciogliersi 788, 1770
sciopero (lo) 2851
sciroppo (lo) 2901
sciupato 2575
scivolare 1153, 2688
scivolo (lo) 2683
scodella (la) 324
scogliera (la) 2379
scoiattolo (lo) 2783

scolaro (lo) 2856
sconsiderato 441
scontento 3128
scontrarsi 579, 659
scontro (lo) 580
scopa (la) 357
scopare 2890
scoppiare 387
scoppio (lo) 269
scoprire 780
scordarsi 1052
scorrere 1031
scorticatura (la) 2535
scorza (la) 2424
scossa (la) 2608
scottare 2514
scricciolo (lo) 3311
scrivania (la) 751
scrivere 3316
scrivere a macchina
    3119
scrivere lettera per
    lettera 2748
scrofa (la) 2736
scudo (lo) 2598
sculacciare 2740
scultore (lo) 2542
scuola (la) 2526
scuola secondaria (la)
    1330
scuotere 2579
scusare 919
scusarsi 81
se 1422
secchio (il) 368, 1994
secolo (il) 476
seconda colazione (la)
    1706
secondo (il) 2554
sedano (il) 469
sedere 2653
sedia (la) 482
sedia a dondolo (la)
    2445
sedia a rotelle (la) 3249
sedile (il) 2551
sega (la) 2509
sega a motore (la) 481
segale (la) 2482
segare 2510

segatura (la) 2511
segnalare 2639
segnale di stop (il)
    2829
segnare 1737, 2532
segreto (il) 2555
seguire 1042
sei 2654
selciato (il) 2051
sella (la) 2486
selvaggio 3268
semaforo (il) 3048
sembrare 2559
seme (il) 2558
semicerchio (il) 2563
seminare 2737
seminterrato (il) 186,
    471
semplice 2645
sempre 59
sempreverde 913
sentenza (la) 2566
sentiero (il) 2046
sentinella (la) 2567
sentire 1293
sentire la mancanza
    1807
sentirsi bene 973
sentirsi soffocare 523
senza scosse 2704
separare 2732
separato 78
sequestrare 1332, 1521
serbatoio (il) 2405, 2927
serpente (il) 2707
serpente a sonagli (il)
    2350
serpentina (la) 573
serra (la) 1200
serratura (la) 1677
servire 2569
sesto 2655
sette 2570
settembre (il) 2568
settimana (la) 3232
settimo 2571
sfera (la) 2750
sforzare 2839
sfrecciare 3335
sfregiare 2675

sgabello (lo) 2827
sgelare 2965
sgraziato 137
sguazzare 2761
shampoo (lo) 2581
sì 3326
sia...che 315
sicomoro (il) 2900
sicuro 2876
sicuro di sè 610
siepe (la) 1300
sigaretta (la) 531
sigaro (il) 530
signora (la) 1556
silenzioso 2641
sindaco (il) 1754
singolare 2647
sinistra (la) 1609
sirena (la) 1774, 2651
siringa (la) 2011
skateboard (lo) 2658
slitta (la) 2677
slittare 2663
slogarsi 2769
smontare 2911
smussato 293
snello 2684
soccorrere 34, 2404
sofà (il) 2719
soffiare 290
soffice 2720
soffitta (la) 124
soffitto (il) 467
soglia (la) 2983
sogliola (la) 2722
sognare 820
sogno (il) 819
solaio (il) 1681
solco (il) 2481
soldato (il) 2721
sole (il) 2868
solitario 1684
solleticare 2994
sollevare 1297, 1636,
    2103, 2340
solo 51, 1684
sonaglio (il) 2349
sonnecchiare 810
sopra 3
soprabito (il) 1976